Through the Mousehole:
A Journey in Faith

Jane Segerstrom

Through the Mousehole:
A Journey in Faith

by Jane Segerstrom

TRIAD PRESS
a division of Triad Interests, Inc.
10811 Riverview Drive
Houston, TX 77042
(713) 978-7212 phone
(713) 789-0424 fax

ISBN 0-936740-20-5

Contents

The Parable

A mouse hole – that tiny, gnawed opening in the base-board of an abandoned house – resembles a parable of **The Entrance to the Kingdom of Heaven**.

Once I believed the Heavenly Kingdom was accessed through tall golden doors where saints walk proudly – wearing virtue as a laurel wreath – after a lifetime of goodness.

I've since discovered the Door to the Kingdom of Heaven is invisible to those standing tall. The door is so tiny and low it can only be glimpsed when one has been flattened by adversity, when resources are exhausted, when hope has fled.

If you are depressed, distraught and at the bottom, rejoice. Open your eyes. You lie before the Door to the Kingdom...new life awaits.

What is the cost of admission? Everything you possess, for nothing but your worthlessness can enter with you.

What do you find on the other side? Ah, what one woman found...

...you'll discover as you read.

1

〜

The Business
Transaction

Slumped on my bed in a still-strange rented house in
the woods of Ohio, I agreed to the most outrageous
business contract one can imagine.

I was sick and alone in the room. No telephone.
Low lamp light bathed my bed, but the walls and ceiling were dark, and the windows had become black mirrors. A branch scratched softly. Except for my sleeping
children and reading husband, no one was within miles.

For more than a year I'd been limp from anemia –
no sparks of energy, spirit or even virtue. My pride, used
to a diet of accomplishments, was starved. I felt flattened – no accomplishments, no value. The weight of

my worthlessness grew daily. Sick, tired, I couldn't go on.

You already know with whom I spoke, prayed, meditated.

I'd tried to be His "good" girl, to do all I should, to shun all things evil. Yet here I was, at thirty-five, physically, emotionally and spiritually bankrupt. That night I closed the account.

"Please help me," I prayed.

A deep, kind voice asked without sound, "Do you want me more than you want *yourself?*"

"Yes, oh yes, I hate me this way." I responded, and then slowly realized the enormity of my assent.

I had just surrendered my right to plan and control my life. I had placed my future in hands which I'd never seen. How could I know I'd not be hurt? I couldn't know it, I reasoned, this has to be an act of faith, not knowledge.

And wasn't God's matchless love, total good? He wouldn't hurt me, I tried to assure myself. And then I remembered my new Christian friend and relaxed. Ginnie loved me and accepted me totally, undisturbed by my imperfections. Was God any less loving and accepting? He couldn't be.

Did I wish to back out? No. I'd already wasted thirty-five years. I'd squandered my health and my talents. Since I had nothing of merit to show from my years of struggle – a spark of challenge ignited in me –

I'd give Him the tiller of my life and see what He could do with it.

Would my challenge annoy the Speaker? No. The atmosphere still comforted me.

"Do you want me more than you want your *marriage?*"

Whoa. I love my husband. He's a good man. We'd been a team for fifteen years. Admittedly, our relationship wore patches and hadn't deepened as I'd hoped, but I'd never considered jettisoning it.

But then I realized having a "Christian Fanatic" as a wife would be intolerable for ultra-conservative Cliff. And I didn't know how fanatical I might become. What a frightening thought. I might find myself on street corners asking strangers the state of their souls, ministering to lepers or serving as a missionary in China.

I obviously couldn't be God's woman without surrendering my marriage to Him. I surrendered it with the belief it would soon be over and with mourning, trusted God to set the time and way.

Again the voice, "Do you want me more than your *children?*"

At only eleven and ten they were still babies. How could I betray a mother's trust, turn my back on them? But then I saw clearly that without God I had nothing of value to offer them. And being Love Itself and Parent to us all, He surely loved them more fully and sanely than I ever could. My response could only be, "Yes, Lord."

"Do you want me more than your *shape?* Are you willing to be fat for me?"

Ouch. I'd fought the scales forever, hovering always ten to twenty pounds away from my goal. If I say, "Yes," I'll become a blimp, waddle down the street, have to pry myself from chairs. "Please don't ask this," I prayed, but the question still echoed within me.

"Yes, yes, even this, Lord," I wept.

"Do you want me more than your *career?*"

Before I became ill I'd taught in a California adult education program. When we returned to California I planned to earn my master's degree before applying for a position to manage the same adult program. This seemed possible, practical and was my big dream. The prospect of giving up teaching and turning away from the status and kudos of my profession was less painful than I expected. And yet, spending the rest of my life without this source of "Brownie Points" hurt. Could I? My answer was, "Yes".

"Do you want me more than your *creativity?*"

You're hitting below the belt, Lord. You know how much my sewing, knitting, writing, singing mean to me. Surely you don't mean to take away my last area of self-justification. Without this I have no value.

"Your value lies in being My daughter, Little One, not in puny efforts. You are royalty...the daughter of the King."

Put that way, how could I refuse? I didn't. "Yes, Lord, I want you more."

How naked I felt, stripped of all which had defined me. No health, shape, family, job, future plans, creative outlets. No, money hadn't been mentioned, but I knew it was included as surely as if it had been stated.

That night I pledged myself to a faceless future – knowing only, trusting only, in the One to whom I'd made my commitment. I'd exchanged my right to myself for what would be a vast emptiness were it not warmed by love and peace.

"Please explain our new relationship, Lord. It would help realign my thinking, help me understand."

The voice was gentle and kind, but the words were firm.

"As a result of bankrupting your 'business' of Jane Segerstrom, Inc., you've resigned as owner/CEO and transferred all stock and control into My hands. I am the new owner/CEO. From now on I'll do the planning and supply the resources. All credit/blame for your actions will belong to Me.

"As my 'Girl-Friday' you'll be free of responsibility for results, but sitting-in on every transaction. You'll change and observe change in others, participating when and how I direct, accomplishing My goals."

"Yes, Boss. But how will I know what you want of me? Can't I have rules? I'm frightened without them."

"Ah, little one, I'll give you rules, even as parents supply a night light for a beloved child who is fearful of the dark. You don't need them but they'll make you feel safer. But these rules are designed for you alone. Other seekers may require different guidelines from those I give you. You may share your joy with them, but when they ask for direction, send them to Me. At times My directions may appear to violate my laws, but they don't. Trust them and Me.

"Your first rule is, *Do always what you want; never what you should,* because you need to turn inward for direction. You've never looked within but have wasted years living by 'shoulds'. You've wasted hours on minor, boring projects. Your only glimpses of Me have been at a great distance, but I want you close. Trust Me to monitor your desires, to block those which are outside my will. Your desires will equal My will. I won't fail you.

"Your second and last rule is to *Keep Me first.* Whenever you want anything, no matter how worthy, more than you want me, you destroy our relationship. The good is enemy of the best. Check your values at each **Y** in the road. You'll know My way if you: first, surrender the choice to Me; then, follow the path your desire uncovers."

"Lord, am I to leave *law* behind with the rest of my valuables? I need law to control me. What if I hurt others? blunder? destroy? You're turning a monster loose!"

"Have no fear, little one, I will always consider your direction. But as a wise parent, I shan't always block your foolish or false words and actions. Trying and failing is a part of your education. Trust Me. The only person hurt will be you – in the ego."

"How can I be sure I won't hurt others? How can you stop me?"

"You forget My resources. I shall check you by circumstances. Accept, don't fight them. I shall place knowledge in your mind when you pray or will use the voice of friends or words of authors. I shall sometimes speak to you as I speak now, using an ever softer voice so you may learn to listen. Lastly, should I need your attention, My voice can transmit to you through every barrier – even time and space – with such volume you'll be stunned. You'll never be able to stop your ears from my voice should I choose that you hear.

"Good night, my child. Tomorrow begins a peaceful new life. Enjoy."

I felt safe, free and surprisingly sleepy. With a smile in my voice, "Goodnight, Boss," I murmured.

2

The Tightrope

Peace cocooned me in the days which followed, strange days – unlike any I had ever known. I felt both totally captive and totally free. My captivity was to God and the discipline he had given me. My freedom was from duties, responsibilities and the need to plan.

The momentous events of 'that' night were too personal, too foreign, too full of wonder to instantly share. Besides, I didn't want to yet, and didn't my new code forbid my doing anything I didn't want to do?

Upon awakening each morning, I questioned myself to see if I preferred to stay abed or get up. Would I make the family's breakfast or read a book? Dress or stay in my robe? Everything had become possible. Since family and doctor had both urged me to rest more, it appeared I might finally take their advice.

To my surprise I often chose to stay in bed, or go back to bed – even several times a day. Previously, I'd hated not having the energy to leave my bed and fretted every moment I lay there.

During the week my family left before dawn and returned after dark. Cliff was project manager on a plant being built in the area and spent long hours at the construction site. John and Carol climbed first on the school bus and last off in their journey to and from a country school. Our temporary residence sat in the middle of a seventeen acre forest – no neighbors. I was alone but strangely not lonely during those long quiet days.

What filled my hours? Expectancy, quiet joy, and the melancholy of loss. I'd surrendered some vague 'pro' status to accept the unfamiliar role of novice. I didn't know how to live this way.

Nothing ran by remote control anymore. Each action had to be deliberately chosen; old habits had to die and new ones develop. Being reprogrammed hurt, but not as much as being what I had been.

I spent the days resting and dozing, reading and dabbling at random jobs. Dishes didn't any longer follow meal preparation. They were washed when I wanted to wash them, dried sometime later, and put away when, or if, I wanted to do that job. Often they sat all day in the dish drainer.

One day I went back to bed five times. I knew friends would be joining us for dinner; but each time I checked, bed held more appeal than any task. It seemed illogical, yet that evening I stayed up past eleven for the first time in a year, felt good, and awoke the next morning surprisingly refreshed. After the fact the extra rest made sense.

I, who had always hated mopping the floor, supposed I'd never mop floors again. Not so. Even that hated duty became something I really wanted to do. Mopping eventually outweighed sticking-to-the-floor.

Long bubble baths became a daily ritual. I felt utterly pampered, luxuriating in them – the Queen of Sheba with a dozen handmaidens. I was surprised to see my hair receive more care, my toenails and fingernails wear multiple coats of polish. I, who had always been last after husband, children and duty had become first.

With the thought I was becoming selfish, guilt bit deep. Yet instantly came the words, "You are my child, the daughter of the King, and guilt is forbidden you. Neither guilt nor fear may abide in you for both are denials of My power. Guilt is a denial of My ability to forgive; fear, a denial of My omnipotence. When either guilt or fear first touch your mind, turn your thoughts to Me. I will banish them."

"Yes, Lord." And then I thought of the exquisite torture I had often put myself through after a party. Why had I made a stupid remark to her? Why had I kept still and not defended him? How could I have been so clumsy? Whoa. I suddenly realized flaying myself over "if only's" gave me a perverse pleasure. I'd miss this form of guilt. Must I give it up? I must. I couldn't subject the daughter of the King to such sick cruelties. She/I was worth more than that.

What happens when I botch things, for I obviously still do? I ask God to forgive me then ask forgiveness of those involved.

But what of fear? I was afraid of snakes, dogs, pain, embarrassment, loss of limb, loss of loved ones, loss of money, loss of sanity. But my greatest fear had become loss of my new relationship to God. Were any fears necessary to me? No. I could be free of fear in His hands.

What happens when the plane loses an engine over Guatemala, the hurricane heads for us in Houston, or I'm out-of-air forty feet below the surface of the Caribbean? I let Him bring me safely to the ground, to clear weather or to the surface of the sea. He won't let me be taken before His appointed time for me.

Across the years I have lived free from guilt and fear. Their siren-calls still beckon me, but they are gone the instant I turn to HIM. My dreams are sweet, nonthreatening.

And the "shoulds" in me became stilled as well. Before, no matter what I did, inner voices scolded me for not doing something else. If I sewed, I should be cooking. If I cleaned, I should be spending time with the children. If I worshipped at church I should be home. I couldn't win.

Now I can do what I want to do, under HIS direction, and feel not only contentment but joy.

My role in handling our family's correspondence was over, I realized, for my frequent letters and notes had been motivated by duty. But after a few weeks I found myself wanting to talk with family and friends, so I wrote them whenever I wished.

The books I read were chosen for me, via my desire, and both the amount read and the rereading seemed perfectly monitored, deliberately rationed. To my delight a number of Christian books appeared in my hands. I'd read the Bible regularly but never before touched contemporary literature about faith. What joy, to learn others had taken unknown paths similar to mine. I felt like the first moon-walker suddenly encountering a gang of "friendlies", similarly employed.

To my surprise, novels became as important to my reading program as "worthy" books. They still are.

To my utter astonishment, Bible reading and a separate devotional time were dropped from my daily routine. When I asked a scandalized, "Why?", I heard, "You have taken pride in your virtue. But no more. No longer may you pat yourself on the back as being a Bible reading, devout, Sunday School teacher. You are allowed no visible virtue. You and I know you are MINE, but it is through MY grace, not your deeds."

My devotional time since then has been spontaneous – over the ironing board, or relaxing in the tub. My days are often filled with continuous praise and thanksgiving. He finds my parking places, teaches me patience at traffic lights, fills me with peace when I must wait. He opens me to the most unlikely people and closes me to those whom I would have chosen as confidants.

This isn't to suggest I'm always open and tuned to our Lord. I'm not. I too often slip into a management-by-Jane mode without noticing, absentmindedly removing my earphones to His voice. Loneliness, failure and dissatisfaction flick me into returning for recentering. Thankfully, His love and forgiveness are unlimited, so I'm again enfolded. That I didn't mean to leave Him is apparent to us both, but it hurts none-the-less. He loans me perfection for a moment, a page, a job, a person, but it never becomes mine.

Only one semester have I taught church school in the thirty years since that night. My inner voice approved; but to my sorrow, team-teaching with set curriculum and completely structured time gave me little opportunity to share the nature of God – the reality of faith – with those wonderful fifth graders. I've not volunteered again.

Regular Bible reading has never been returned, but the scriptures memorized in childhood often come to mind with new meaning and clarity. Although my new discipline replaced Biblical law, *it has never led me to violate it.*

Amazed, I see how He reinterpreted His two great laws for me: *Thou shalt love the Lord thy God with all thy heart, and with all thy soul, and with all thy mind;* and *Thou shalt love thy neighbor as thyself.* Doing only what I want, has been God's tool for teaching me to love myself. Loving my neighbor wasn't possible until I could love me.

Why, I wondered, did the Father draw me and not His Son by whom most others are drawn? But then I knew. As a child I didn't look to my peers for approval but strove to be a good little girl whom parents and teachers would admire. Yes, a "Goodie-Two-Shoes." Since authority figures had the greatest importance, God reached me through His Father presence.

A Christian friend once told me I followed the God of Abraham. It seems true. I walk a strange land by His guidance.

Does this mean I don't believe in Jesus, the Christ? Absolutely not. By His life, death and resurrection He made this new life possible. He bridged the distance sin placed between God and me. Jesus built the communication system by which I hear. He's my elder brother who understands my foibles, loves me and pleads my case.

Only later did I recognize my comforting, teaching, inner voice is God the Holy Spirit. Being this loved by all Three is beyond comprehension. The truth of it grips my heart and brings tears to my eyes.

The GUIDE with whom I travel and by whom I'm taught grows daily more dear. It would be pleasant to believe my prowess at walking in faith has grown with the years. But not so. I'm still a novice at faith and love. His gift of grace supports me. When I turn away, I stumble and fall, virtueless.

In the beginning it seemed as though I had stepped away from familiar, solid ground and onto a tightrope which stretched off into infinity. I could see only dimly, for mists obscured all directions beyond the space ahead for just one foot. I balanced precariously, not knowing how to walk a tightrope. I couldn't see how this one was secured, nor where it led me. But I knew turning around and going back had become impossible for two reasons: nothing in my previous life held value, and I couldn't turn around without falling away from Him.

God supplied both the rope and my balance. My job was to trust HIM for the steadiness and strength to take the next step.

I've been taking single steps toward an unknown destination ever since. The path I've followed has been circuitous, often doubling back on itself, with no discernable destination, but it's been lit with love and miracles. I trust the One who guides me.

I'm living an adventure story. Hallelujah!

3

*Clocks and
Calendars*

Days felt chartless – without recognizable form. Stripped of goals, I drifted as would a sailor in a dinghy without oars, charts, compass or sextant.

Never was I told to leave my watch upon the dresser, but my hand was stopped each time I reached for it. Never was I forbidden to glance at the clock, but my mind was always distracted whenever I would peek.

Time had previously structured my life. Would I never have structure again? Apparently not.

I had been transported into a foreign world, an ancient one, where day was heralded by the sun, and night by the stars and moon.

Never before had I eaten by "tummy" time. Two-hands-on-twelve had previously signaled time for lunch. Now I ate whenever, not knowing if it were mid-morning, mid-afternoon, or sometime in between. Eating whatever I wanted, whenever, was novel.

It seemed impossible that I, who had felt fat since birth, was free of dieting. Food tasted better than ever now there was time to savor each mouthful; yet, to my surprise, I didn't grow fatter. Excessive weight didn't come then, nor has it come since.

In answer to your unvoiced question...no, I'm not reed thin. Along with most women I have rounded curves. But unlike many, my former obsession with weight and food has been transformed into a more comfortable self-acceptance. Am I ever saddened by my reflection in the mirror? Of course. I'm not unaware I differ from the broad shouldered, narrow hipped, long legged boy-women favored today. But then, my shape was sculpted for me by our Maker. Since He stated his work was good, how dare I complain?

I'd never before read, then reread, a few pages in a book and mulled them for hours – feeling the balance of the pages to be a treat reserved for later, not for now.

I'd never had time to watch birds and squirrels from my windows. To note the difference in exquisite light on leaves in early morning, at noon and as the dying sun warmed them. I'd never strolled leisurely through fall's crispness, crunching colorful leaves underfoot and smelling the wood smoke.

My world was a new and unfamiliar place to be tasted, smelled, heard, touched and explored. A fresh snowfall sparkled on trees and bushes one morning, transforming the familiar into a silent fairyland of brilliance and heart-stopping beauty. The outside world had been cleansed and transformed just as had God's work in me.

But the most exciting difference was in my attitude toward people – especially my children and husband. I'd always 'done' for them but never really 'been there' for them.

Before, people were intrusions, keeping me from marking off completed project. Phone calls were interruptions, visitors unwelcome, my family a necessary evil.

Now Cliff and the children had become God's responsibility, not mine, so I was free to enjoy them, to listen, to share. Besides, I reasoned, I may not have them close much longer. They're His now; they aren't mine to keep. Like library books, they're only on loan to me. I didn't know when we'd be parted, but I expected it shortly.

With such long open days I couldn't wait for John and Carol to arrive home from school. They still speak of the day I held a tea party on the floor for the three of us when they had trudged up the hill.

They seemed surprised and delighted when I would join them at Ping-Pong while before I'd always declined with, "I'm too busy," or "I'm too tired." Being more of a klutz than a whiz, I brought little to the game except what was most important – the clear message, I loved them; they counted large in my life.

Dinners, often improvisations with everyone helping, were festive with a mother at the table who wasn't gray with fatigue. And because I had seen the fluffy gray squirrel with nuts in both cheeks, remembered a comment our daughter made about school, and had listened to our son practice his clarinet, I had more interesting conversation to offer.

When my husband asked about my improved mood, I told him and the children about the deep recommitment I'd made to God. I said I was learning to live a new way. Since they asked few questions, elaboration wasn't necessary.

One Friday, a few months later, I was given a memorable lesson about time. We had returned to our home near Los Angeles, but for months Cliff worked near San Francisco and came home only on weekends. This Friday I expected him home in time for us to entertain friends at dinner.

I presumed since I had cleaning and cooking to do that day, I'd begin one or the other of those activities while it was early. Not so.

My first act of the day was to walk into the sunshine, stretch and begin weeding the planter box. This wouldn't surprise except I've always hated weeding. Yet, for half an hour all I wanted to do was weed.

The next half hour was spent in picking out one-finger melodies on my husband's organ. After that I read a chapter in a novel, sewed a button on a shirt, thumbed through a magazine, made myself a delightful salad and consumed it on our deck.

Sound peaceful? Yes. Was it? No. War was raging inside me. I'd committed myself to doing only what I wanted to do, and that's what I followed; but the things I *needed* to do screamed louder and louder, demanding attention. The temptation to trade God's discipline for duty was at an all-time high. "Why can't *some* of the things I *have* to do be allowed me?", I fumed. "When, Lord, can we quit this playing around and get down to business?" I queried. The words, "Get thee behind me, Satan." popped into my mind.

By four in the afternoon I'd resigned myself to a dirty house and a pick-up dinner for guests. Yet soon I found myself with mop in hand leisurely cleaning the floor – the first appearance of any logical activity. By six-thirty I was bathed and dressed, the house looked fine – not to say was clean – and dinner preparations were on-schedule. I greeted Cliff and our guests and was assured by all I looked great – more rested than they'd seen me in some time.

The clock figured prominently in one additional lesson. I lay down to rest one afternoon, but couldn't allow myself to doze because of a late afternoon appointment. Resetting the alarm clock was a logical solution, but I opted to ask God to awaken me instead. Not yet secure, I asked God a second time to please awaken me by 3:00 p.m. And just before I dozed, I reminded Him I was counting on Him. Yes, I was the one with little faith.

At two minutes to three I awakened, crisply alert. Within the next three minutes the telephone rang twice and someone rang the doorbell. Coincidence? I think not. Since I'd repeated my request three times, He answered my prayer thrice. Who says God hasn't a sense of humor?

Not surprisingly, the calendar also became a teaching tool to show me God's grace. My old calendar had been so crammed I was squeezed; while my new calendar held empty space.

I floated into activities as though a current carried me lazily along. I'd check to see if I wanted to try something others proposed, and unless I didn't want to, it was simpler to accept. Swimming against the current was out – it appeared.

And choosing activities differently has netted new enthusiasm, new friendships, new opportunities and a new peace.

God maneuvers me by circumstances. Some activities can't be attended because of prior commitments. As His daughter, I can't hedge after my word is given. Besides, God, knowing the future, could have kept me from accepting if He'd wanted me elsewhere. He wants me there.

When family ski trips first threatened church time, His message came through loud and clear, I couldn't use perfect church attendance as a source of spiritual pride. He wanted us to be with Him on the slopes.

Cliff repeatedly tried to arrange our return trip from Ohio to California to allow us to ski with our California ski club the week they'd be at Alta, Utah. We missed their dates, returning through the Rockies a week later.

Our ski club had been so snowed-in they couldn't even ski. Due to avalanche danger, slopes were closed for the entire week. They had to ski out, fly home, then return later for cars and campers. We, however, found beautiful powder at Vail and Aspen and few skiers. News of the storm had kept others away. Those days on the slopes made red-letter memories for our family.

Requests for monetary and time donations once filled checkbook and calendar. Formerly I'd weigh each request intellectually. Those deemed worthy received a, "Yes," and I made room for them somehow, performing them with a martyr's sigh.

My new discipline keeps me from answering any request until I have weighed whether or not I passionately want to do it. If I don't, I decline.

Guilt instantly flicks me with, "You're doing NOTHING, and this was a valuable activity. How can you turn her down and still call yourself a Christian?"

Time and again the guilt has been melted by God's presence. I repeat as a litany, "It's far harder to do nothing for God than something for Him." I know I'll be stressed until 'pride in my Father' permanently replaces 'pride in my accomplishments.'

A princess doesn't have to justify her royalty. She gains it at birth. Her father is THE KING. My job is to accept being His daughter and to worship the King.

And a side effect – when time had passed, I found fascinating projects came along which I was dying to do. Because my calendar was clear, I could say, "Yes," with joy. Because each was done enthusiastically, God's results became remarkable.

Each vacation, each luncheon engagement, each business transfer – even the one which took us to Holland for eighteen months – has to pass His interior check in me. As long as I follow this system I stay 'in synch.'

Conversely, whenever I'm determined to have my way, I'm not only miserable but make those around me miserable. Seeing others turn-off when I'm around is evidence I need God's forgiveness for leaving Him. I give Him back myself and return the calendar to His keeping.

When acquaintances say they would phone me sometime or stop by to see me but are afraid I'm too busy, I laughingly answer, "God keeps my calendar. If you need me, I'm sure to be free."

4

Lists, Phones
and Scales

All my lifetime habits appeared one-by-one before me for reevaluation under God's guidance. Not surprisingly, my lists were the first thing I tried to justify.

Lists had kept me sharp. They held my pre-selected goals – rank ordered by importance. They buffered a poor memory and kept me on track. Marking each completed project off the day's list was my pat-on-the-back. How could I function without lists? I felt naked.

At the time I couldn't see, but later it became plain the lists I'd valued so highly had ceased to be helpers. They'd become killers. Each day was so crammed with

activity that even running faster and faster I got farther and farther behind. I'd hated myself for not being
able to complete each day's duties. Then, because I
didn't deserve better, I'd added even more items to
tomorrow's list. Lists became symptoms of my illness,
my addiction. In today's terms, I am a recovering
workaholic.

Released from the hold of lists, I was directionless,
lacking purpose, going through withdrawal. I was a
house swept clean into which something, or someone,
would surely move.

"Give me purpose, Lord," I prayed.

"Here is the greatest purpose, my child. Just praise
Me and love Me forever."

"Only this, Lord God?"

"Only this, my child."

Today various projects nest in my head and on my
desk, but I work on only those which appear most in-
viting. Deadlines for completion, if any, are supplied
by others, not by me. Goal setting, as recommended by
every speaker, is impossible. How can I strive to reach
a destination when only God knows where I'm going?
He, wisely, shows me only individual steps – no wide
panoramas.

I didn't realize at the beginning the telephone had
entered this new realm with me. To my amazement,
calls became direct answers to my needs for friendship,

information or feeling needed. They became positive – not negative, sought – not dreaded.

Incoming calls also came at perfect times – when I had nothing important to do or needed a break from intense effort. Outgoing calls became delayed until my interior guidance flashed a green light. I'm certain God still monitors my phone's switchboard.

One morning I awoke with a divine message for a husband I was informally counseling whose wife was my friend. I wanted desperately to phone George, but my personal code for working with men was that I never contact them. They must contact me. I prayed he would phone, but the phone didn't ring, and my urgency didn't cease.

At last I could bear it no longer and picked up the phone. "Please have him gone or his line busy, Lord, if it isn't You who initiated this," I prayed.

George answered on the first ring and listened to my message. His response was he'd prayed specifically for an answer to that problem at the exact time I'd awakened. He had almost lost hope on having a reply, thinking God hadn't responded to his despair. He thanked me with tears for delivering God's message.

I, ashamed, apologized to both George and God for the delay. My stubborn control and lack of faith had blocked His speedy reply.

How did scales come into my growth? They weigh merchandise, of course, but also decisions. The choices most commonly weighed by the worldly are good and evil. But as Christians committed to good, our choices are more subtle – between the good and the best. Ours become questions of motivation.

When a checker in the grocery store undercharged me, I showed her the error. This wasn't new behavior for me, but it was from a new motive. Previously I'd been honest because it was the law. Without the law, I discovered I'm honest because it is my nature – God's nature in me.

When a host offered wine at a party, a quick interior check confirmed I was to take one glass. 'Good Christians don't drink' was the law being sundered. 'God's people trust God for their individual answer, not laws,' was the message being taught.

When a realtor asked me three separate times what the source was for my radiance, I told him each time, after checking, it was, "Clean living." That I shouldn't share my joy in Christ was unthinkable. I was willing to share it anytime, anywhere. When I asked my Inner Guidance, "Why should I be so muzzled?" the answer came back through scripture. "Cast not your pearls before swine." I'd never have thought he met that description.

Happily, I am allowed to share my spiritual life with select friends, total strangers and the most unlikely prospects – at most unusual times. Witness is something God does, through me, to those He chooses. When I try to witness alone, I embarrass both myself and the recipient. He saves His seed for prepared soil.

Witnessing apparently comes in two parts: the words to share and the opportunity in which to share them.

At first I blasted an opening for my news immediately upon receiving the words. Wrong. My words weren't heard. "Why, Lord?"

"Wait for the opportunity, my child. I will prepare an opening which is large enough to drive a truck through. Wait until you see the opening before you deliver My message. No matter how long, wait on Me. Then My words will be heard."

I'm forbidden to bake an apple pie with no more justification than that my husband loves it. When I baked to make him happy, I was needy until he thanked and complimented me for my efforts. As he usually didn't recognize a pie as an extreme gift, he failed to thank or compliment and I felt bruised.

I may only bake when the desire to bake a pie is so strong my full pleasure comes from the act. Then, whether the product is raved over or garbage disposed, I'm content. I make it for my pleasure in the making. Unfortunately for Cliff, I've baked few pies since then, but bakery pies can be tasty, too.

One day I painted the bathroom walls of a house we had just purchased. I felt as if I had become Huck Finn, splotching my jeans, swinging my legs and having a lovely time.

The next day it seemed logical to paint the laundry room, for then we could move equipment in. What a miserable day! I tipped over the paint tray, dropped my brush into the bucket and brushed the wet ceiling with my hair. The paint didn't even spread as well. What changed?

I'd painted the first day for pure love of painting, the second to get the job done. God was reminding me no matter how attractive logic can be, I am to be motivated solely by my desires – not trapped back in the world of duty.

Creativity dies when I try to force it; it blossoms when I'm consumed by the desire to write or paint or design.

"Please continue to remind me of this, Lord."

Taking and giving are another couplet. Giving was easy – I was comfortable with the scales tipped to my side. Taking was painful – I didn't want to be beholden. Learning to accept the gifts of others, the compliments of others, with a gracious, "Thank you", has been one of my most difficult lessons – it's one I'm still learning. And God has heaped upon me so many untold, unearned blessings that I'm in awe and eternally grateful.

Who can say what is good, what evil?

God said the world He made was good. But all around are church folk judging the death of the Arnold baby was bad, Helen and Jake shouldn't be living-together, it's terrible that Barney lost his job, it's a crime Ramona has cancer. Maybe.

Inside me has grown the assurance I don't know what's good or bad, nor do I need to know. God knows, not I, what the Arnold's baby's life would have held had he lived. He alone knows what is in Helen and Jake's heart. He knows just how much pressure is needed for Barney to break, and in breaking, surrender to JOY. He can perhaps use Ramona's cancer to heal her, and those who love her, spiritually – whether she lives or dies.

It seems when we are 'born again' we return to a childlike state which precedes the knowledge of good and evil. We walk in the garden with God, trusting Him for everything, making no judgments of our own. We are in heaven on earth.

Yet in our ears the snake still whispers beguilingly, "Why shouldn't you, also, be a god and sit in judgment? Power and control are yours when you turn from Him."

By accepting adulthood, responsibility for ourselves and others, knowing what is right and wrong, we become Gods in our own right. We eat of the fruit which casts us from God's presence. I lived outside-the-Garden, in sin against God, for the first thirty-five years of my life. I don't recommend it. It represented only failure and was killing me.

Now I yo-yo between the two worlds. Repeatedly – though unconsciously – I bite the apple, hate the me who has lost His love, repent, then gratefully accept again His grace and presence.

But, thankfully, both He and I know where my will lies – firmly with Him in the garden.

5

The Dreaded Question

Daily, the first week of my new life, I braced for the words from my husband, Cliff, which would shatter our marriage.

Wasn't he a conservative, practical engineer, a man who carefully avoided the limelight? Didn't he chose to live protectively, surrounded by acceptable children and an acceptable wife? During the nearly fifteen years of our marriage hadn't I tried to be the woman he wanted, tried to *never rock the boat*?

Then how could he stand for my new allegiance? What would he say? How soon would we be parted?

That we not be parted didn't enter my calculations, for I could see no other way for us. All I could do was to trust God with our future, believing He would have the words I should speak when the time came.

My body relaxed on the bed while my mind drifted back across the years of our marriage...

We'd met as freshmen in college, freshman week, on a blind date rigged by our respective roommates. They were "going steady", and Cliff had a car. Any success of our first date – to see the football team off to a pre-season game – was totally due to the other couple. Neither Cliff nor I could find common ground.

His world was cars and sports; mine was books and philosophy. He was a jock, I a bookworm. Childhood asthma had benched me from sports.

He was tall and trim, well coordinated, with light-blue eyes and red-blond hair; I was short-average and rounded, somewhat klutzy, with green eyes and ash-brown hair.

Cliff and I were matched in being non-gorgeous, prompt, truthful, and church attenders. Our parents attended church, our fathers worked for utility companies, our mothers worked only at home. We both had limited funds and, especially that first year, even more limited conversation.

I made notes of overheard anecdotes and jokes in order to share at least one paragraph with him at dinner. Why did we continue to see each other? We both enjoyed the other couple and tolerated the foursome because of them.

We four ate in the dining hall before studying together in the library. On Thursday evenings we played bridge at the dining table of – under the watchful eye of – the fellows' landlady. We attended all the during-the-week sports events. On weekends Cliff went home to his steady girl. I often stayed at school and studied, dating occasionally, disinterestedly.

In late spring Cliff, whom I'd come to care for, called me from home on Saturday morning for a date Sunday night. I declined because of a class deadline. He said, "Please, let me at least take you out for a quick bite. You have to eat." I accepted, smiling, knowing he knew I had dates both Friday and Saturday nights with interesting men.

That evening he asked, "What are you doing Thursday, Friday, Saturday and Sunday of next weekend?" Looking back I can't remember any more romantic words this practical man has ever spoken.

In the late forties-early fifties, good girls stayed good with the assistance of their nice guys. And so, although we steamed up his car during the college years, we married in the spring of '51 before joining ourselves as one.

Why did we marry? It was a badge of success – what people expected of us. Not marrying didn't enter our heads.

Why did we marry each other? I used to believe we just happened to be together at marrying time. I believe now that God chose us to be marriage partners.

Of course both sets of parents firmly believed we'd married beneath us, but each tolerated the new in-law.

He went to work for an oil company. I taught junior high foods until I became pregnant with John. We bought our first home, a new refrigerator and had John within a six week span. Eleven months and five days later we had a daughter, Carol.

Those first five years became a shakedown cruise.

Both being quick and prompt was an unexpected and unbelievable gift. I was delighted my new husband enjoyed maintaining our home and appliances and did so cheerfully. My father hated household maintenance. Cliff built furniture for us – could make anything I could design. He was neat with his things and always looked bandbox fresh. He was faithful, hard working and a good provider. He attended church with me even though he refused to join my church.

I was, however, less than delighted to realize he'd never give me the verbal and nonverbal assurance of his love I craved and expected. My parents verbalized their love and touched.

If only his standards for me hadn't been so high! He expected a spotless house, smiling and fragrant cherubs, delicious meals on time served by a perfect wife and mother. He was an only child reared by two Swedish women – mother and grandmother – dedicated to hearth and home. And I was a professional home economist, after all.

But my parent's home had been a shambles. Projects covered every available surface and only I seemed to care about putting away and cleaning up. I'd never lived in a home such as his, nor he in one such as mine. My comfort level and his were worlds apart.

Cliff wanted a slim, pretty wife he could always be proud of, but he married me. Like my mother, I was far more eager to get the job done than to keep my hair unmussed. She wasn't a model of femininity, neither was I. My makeup, hairstyle, clothing never met approval in his eyes – nor in mine.

He expected meat and potato dinners from the beginning, and despite my college degree I was only learning how to cook. College foods labs supplied knowledge but not practical experience. At home I'd been the table setter, salad maker and dish dryer, period. He enjoyed repetition in his meals; I preferred variety. My early casseroles, expensive in ingredients and time of preparation, auditioned to his look, "What did I do to make you angry?"

It was some time before I recognized I deliberately chose to cook unusual dishes with a high probability of failure. Why? Low self-esteem. Buried deep was the knowledge that making mistakes and eating them anyway was a well-deserved personal punishment. God's solution to my dysfunctional thinking was for me to let Him choose the recipes I should pursue, monitor the making, and leave me free of responsibility for the results. Food has lost most of its emotional impact for me, and Cliff is far happier. Thanks be to God!

The children compounded my problems. Even then I was ill with anemia, dragging myself through those baby days, too tired to stand when folding diapers, too busy to catch my breath. Parenthood then meant washing diapers before hanging them on the clothesline, sterilizing bottles before filling them with sterile formula – no dryer or disposables – no nearby grandmother to lend a hand.

Carol was three before I noticed the sky was blue.

I hated being a nag, but desperately needing assurance of my husband's love, I asked him every six months if he loved me. I kept my questions to that frequency by marking the intervals on the calendar. Cliff's response to this threat was to barricade his gate and raise his drawbridge. I knew it would happen, but I couldn't not ask. I needed to know.

Shortly after our fifth anniversary I told him I needed more emotional support than I was receiving. Would he see a marriage counselor with me? He asked for one more year, promising at the end of that period he'd go with me if things didn't become better. Knowing he was too private to share with an outsider what he couldn't even share with me, I said, "All right."

And then a miracle, the unexpected answer to prayer. The teacher resigned who'd been leading our

"Young Marrieds" class in Sunday School. He was replaced by Dr. R., a young church deacon and practic-
ing psychologist. His topic for the next three years was,
"Marriage Communications."

What I learned was I, the verbal one in this marriage, was primarily responsible for communications.
Whenever I felt something I *must* verbalize those feelings to Cliff, otherwise the unsaid would build in me
until I erupted.

I was to share both the good feelings and the bad,
but I was to be careful how I shared them.

If I attacked with, "Why didn't you...?", I could expect to be attacked right back. If, instead, I said, "When
I see this I feel...," he could respond – or not – without
being threatened.

When I became responsible for only sharing my feelings and freed of trying to ascertain or change Cliff's, I
found release. I knew my telling him I loved him made
him squirm. It did for years. But it made me feel better
for the telling, so I spoke whatever I felt. His reaction
was his responsibility, not mine.

The following example never happened, for Cliff
doesn't slam doors, but I have used it often in talks and
conversations to clarify this tool which has become so
meaningful.

I'm doing the dishes when Cliff lopes past, the door
slamming after him. I've realized for the first time he
continually lets the door slam. It bothers me.

That it bothers me means I have two choices: be silent or speak. If I'm silent, each time the door slams I'll become angrier and angrier until I yell at him about mowing the lawn.

If I speak I'll have either war or peace.

"You're certainly inconsiderate – slamming the kitchen door each time you come in or go out – where did you learn your manners?", will net a similar attack, beginning with, "You're not so perfect yourself." and itemizing my many flaws. That's WAR.

To have peace I speak only about how I feel, never about what Cliff is. "You may think me crazy, but the door's banging makes me jittery. I'm starting to climb the walls.", tells how I feel. It lets Cliff say, "Gee, honey, I'm thinking of something else, not even noticing the door. I'll try to tone it down."

The next time the door slams – only rarely does verbalizing the problem change it – my reaction is different.

If we've had war or I've never expressed by feelings, I'm muttering, "He does it just to annoy me.", my anger spiraling. If we've had peace, I'm thinking, "The big lug, he doesn't even notice. Guess he'll never change."

Should the problem annoy me again, I speak again.

We've hammered out the compromises through the years, but I guess that tool was the single most important communication gift we received.

Are all marriages half-loaves? I wondered. Cliff and I had both settled for less than our dreams. I'd dreamed my husband-to-be would be a stimulating conversationalist. Cliff had dreamed of a bride in pink nail polish who'd cheerfully make and keep his home *perfect*.

What kind of life will he build without me? Happy, I hope. He's a fine man.

I arose from my reverie, refreshed.

Each day flowed without comment – until Sunday. While washing the dishes, Cliff finally spoke, "I want you off this kick. Do you think I can stand having a fanatic for a wife?"

His question floated quietly above my head. I was surprised my primary emotion was relief. The moment that would change my life had arrived.

I calmly reached up to Him for a response and found it to be a question.

"Do you want me the way I was a week ago?", I asked. Cliff answered, "No."

6

⚮

A Strange
Divorce

My journey continued, one tentative step at a time. Cliff didn't voice his opposition, but he seemed to have become a critical observer, tallying the disadvantages of my new stance, threatened by the new me.

We had returned to our Los Angeles area home, and the children had reentered their old school when Cliff was asked to take a temporary assignment. Since he'd be working near San Francisco, it meant either commuting home on weekends or moving the family again. This time we opted to leave the family home and let him commute. What a blessing!

We had married just before Cliff's last semester in college, so he'd never had a chance to live as a bachelor with money in his pocket. He'd never been free to walk at his own pace, to do totally what he wanted to do. Now he had that opportunity.

For eleven months his weekday home was a motel on the marina. He took his tennis racket and began playing several nights a week. Cliff built strong friendships with fellow employees and dined often in their homes. He had needed personal space, personal time, and was refreshed by this new lifestyle.

I also benefitted. Not having a husband home during the week meant the children and I could dine informally, no major meals to prepare. I had extra time in which to practice being the new me.

Because the evenings seemed long, I began something I'd longed to do. I joined the church choir and attended weekly rehearsals. The music was difficult yet absorbing. Cliff even enjoyed having the children to himself in the pew on Sunday mornings while I was in the choir loft. I've sung in the choir everywhere we've lived since then, and he joined the choir, as well, five years later.

A new daytime activity which I'd never previously considered was suddenly attractive. I wanted to learn to play tennis! Public courts with an instructor were near our home, and there, at a group lesson, I found a fellow beginner with similar lack of skill. She and I played singles several times a week. On weekends Cliff and I played mixed doubles with married friends.

Our weekends together were horrible. Cliff and I each brought high expectations for this time, but we had different goals. We acted as if we were spoiled children, each used to having its own way. After a few weeks of pain, we stopped expecting everything of this time, and it took on a more normal aspect. We then enjoyed being together as a family and as a couple.

Transfers to Denver, New York, San Francisco and Houston followed. In Denver my new doctor didn't believe I'd had anemia – my blood would have shown it – so he tested my bone-marrow. There was no trace, no evidence of deficiency. He believed my previous doctor hadn't known his business. I believed, and still do, my previous doctor had a different woman for his patient. The woman I am becoming and the woman I was are totally dissimilar.

By San Francisco, both children attended high school. Cliff had joined me in the church choir, and we both played tennis doubles during the week, mixed doubles on weekends. We swam several times a week and began remodeling our kitchen.

My trusting God totally and following my desires had so far batted a thousand, but then a desire came which shook my composure.

Being a late bloomer and marrying at twenty-one, I had missed the electricity of roving males. It was as though my receiving set had always been on other stations. Now my set had, suddenly, somehow, been switched to their siren song.

Shock. Dismay. This couldn't be, but it was. I desired the same freedom and opportunity to know men as I had to know women. No matter how I checked, that's what I wanted.

"But, I'm married and a Christian," argued my reason.

"Aren't you committed to this walk of faith no matter where it leads you?", queried my Inner Guidance. "Hadn't you expected God to part you from Cliff years ago? Well, it appears the time is here."

That evening I told Cliff I was divorcing him, and why. He was understandably threatened. I was pained to have to hurt him. I found myself explaining my need for release from my marriage vows. I had to be free to follow this new direction – wherever it led me. There was no one else; I didn't know if there ever would be. I promised to keep him totally informed as to my emotional whereabouts. Unless he wished it, I didn't feel the need to leave our home and bed immediately, not unless or until there was someone else.

It was three days later when I made my report. "I left our marriage to explore relationships with men. I find it's a man, not men I want. The man I've settled on, for the time being, is fine and good. You'd like him. He appears in your mirror every morning. Darling, I want a deep, personal relationship with *you*."

Thus began a span of living with my husband because I preferred him to every other man. I didn't retake my marriage vows until we attended a Marriage Encounter Weekend six years later, in Houston.

Looking back I can see the value in this strange divorce where neither of us had been unfaithful in mind or deed.

No longer was I the girl who had chosen Cliff in college nor was he the boy I chose. We had become different people, together from habit and law. God gave us, again, the priceless gift of choice.

Cliff needed to feel valuable, that he was the man I wanted above all others. He was, and still is, that man.

My faith needed this hurdle which seemed to risk our marriage but meant only its healing. I gained insight into the barriers which had lain between us, and the courage to attack them.

Our intellectual and sexual lives had always been fine, but I needed to be held, cuddled and touched – apart from sex. My previous overtures in these areas had consistently been misread as seduction. Foolishly, I had never verbalized exactly what I wanted.

If I was to learn to know this man of mine deeply and personally, I had to open my mouth and arms, to speak and show. I did, and his cool detachment melted. He may rarely tell me he loves me in words, but he's become a master at telling me with his glance, his touch, his caring. He has become a marvelous non-verbal communicator.

One Saturday Cliff was working on the kitchen cabinets while I lay on the living room sofa reading a novel. He, for the third time, asked me for some tool or assistance. I put down my book and crossed the floor to help him, a smile on my lips. I smiled for two reasons: I could at last be content not working when someone else worked, and I could be interrupted this often without irritation.

The sentence, "You are married.", flashed suddenly into my head. What did it mean? I mulled the statement until the answer became clear.

There had been a clause in Cliff's view of our marriage contract which read, "Unless she becomes an embarrassment to me." I'd felt it from the beginning, but it was never spoken or written. Now the clause was gone. We became truly joined – no matter what the future held.

Through the years Cliff has grown to share his feelings with me and with others. Mellowed and softened, he moves whistling through the day, brightening the space around him. He is much loved.

Earlier I mentioned Cliff first watched my new life as a critic, collecting negative data. Later, I realized he was neutral – still watching, listening and weighing – but no longer antagonistic. Still later he was no longer neutral but was in my corner urging me on. Now, without words, I feel him in God's ring with me fighting by my side.

Once, in a marriage class, we were asked to tell each other the three things we liked most about our marriage. I have long since forgotten the words I shared with Cliff but I have never forgotten two of the three things he said to me. He said, "I appreciate your letting me do my own things and enjoy your doing so many things with me."

When God forced me to fight for room to grow, He gave us both the room He cleared. I'm free to travel where I need to, do what I must, without concern for leaving Cliff alone. He, also, is free to pursue his own interests without concern for leaving me alone. He's as competent handling food and clothes as he is with a computer or hammer.

We've come a long way from the times I couldn't leave his side at the television set while he was watching a program.

Today, skiing, tennis and square dancing are no longer on our calendar, but he plays golf and we exercise, play bridge, scuba, take underwater and nature photographs, sing in the choir and worship God--together.

We are in our mid-sixties, but we descend the choir stairs hand-in-hand. We've been married forty-five years, but we're newly in love, and very grateful for this precious gift from Him.

Long ago we settled for a half-a-loaf relationship, but God didn't intend His children to live so. He remade us so our loaf might be rich, full and whole. It overflows the pan.

7

Building Airplanes

We eagerly awaited our first child. Resting, walking and eating as directed became my focus. I read good books and Dr. Spock so he, or she, might begin life with every advantage. I thought I was prepared.

But when John was laid in my arms, I was dumbfounded; the long anticipated Mother's Love didn't engulf me. I had to learn to love this tiny, perfect life. Was I unnatural?

That I was John's mother made me no better at diapering him the first time than was his father; we both brought inexperience to the task. Parenthood bestowed no instant gifts, emotional or physical, but it gave us the wondrous reality of a new life to care for.

I was tired and overwhelmed by responsibility. John was switched from breast to bottle at one month – insufficient milk. At two months he began to sleep through the night. At three months I was pregnant again.

We'd wanted two children, fifteen months apart – after I had taught for two years. John came too soon for me to complete my second year. Carol appeared eleven months and five days later. Eager children, these.

John took his first steps while I was in the hospital with Carol. He felt proud of, and responsible for, his tiny sister and helped me with her as much as he could.

Neither Cliff nor I were the gifted parents we'd thought we'd be. We had a limited store of gentle words and patience. We had a limited income, too, because we'd borrowed the down payment for our house and thus repaid two loans at once. My anemia compounded our problems, but we basically didn't enjoy the responsibility of little children. Each year we did, however, enjoy them more.

Neighbors shaped our opinions about child rearing. On the south a thrice-married woman's teenage son, by an early marriage, occasionally visited. She paid his fines, retired his loans and slipped him money she needed for herself. He called her X-rated words.

On the north lived a German couple with a teen-age son who had earned his own money since he was twelve. This young man was a dutiful son, a responsible citizen and a hard worker. Much was expected of him, and he met expectations with high grades.

We would expect much from our children and love them much – as much as we could.

John was a cuddler. Being held and stroked and sung to were fun. He openly shared his joys and sorrows and held up his "ouches" to be kissed away.

When John was 29, he shared the most enlightening moment of his childhood, an event I had long forgotten.

Five-year-old John had left the neighbors, where he had permission to play, and was returning home when he found a stub of colored chalk. Seeing the sidewalk near our home as an entrancing canvas, he drew a grand picture, not noticing the mess he was making. When he'd finished his masterpiece, he was struck by guilt. What should he do?

He decided he'd tell Mother. She'd probably punish him, but even that would be better than the pain he was suffering from worry and guilt.

When I correctly read his deep remorse and didn't scold him but helped him wash away the evidence, he realized my love wasn't conditional. It was there for him no matter what he did. I didn't fail him then, but I somehow failed Carol.

Tiny Carol didn't want to be held or cuddled by her father or me. Instead she bonded herself to John and became his inseparable companion. She seemed happy to be trotting at John's heels. Carol enjoyed both rollicking activity and quiet play, but she kept her thoughts hidden from her parents. For several years the only contact she allowed me was sharing her piano bench, helping her learn her pieces.

Carol's piano teacher said, "Your daughter can become a gifted pianist if she works hard daily on each assigned lesson." Carol did. But when we moved, her new piano teacher demanded no practice, no loyalty to the instrument, and Carol quit the piano. Unfortunately, she has never gone back.

Carol was a good child, if stubborn. When tiny she'd reach again and again for the forbidden. I was almost relieved the day she managed to slip a key into an electrical outlet plate without being hurt. I had warned repeatedly that the baseboard plates were "hot" but she didn't believe it until one sparked and tingled her hand.

With two small children, I counted Sunday mornings as the worst time of the week. I couldn't get the family fed, the dishes done, the children and myself dressed and still be at church on time – no matter when I set the alarm. I shared my dilemma with God and then Cliff. My husband thereafter voluntarily cooked Sunday breakfast and cleaned up afterwards. Once again prayer was the key. I could look forward to Sunday's promised in-filling. We peacefully worshipped together as a family.

Later, school mornings became difficult, and Cliff left too early to help. Getting John and Carol dressed, fed and on the school bus took more "push" than I had available.

A little prayer and the solution became clear. I would resign from the responsibility of getting them to school and place it on their shoulders and God's. We bought each an alarm clock and laid out their clothing at night. John and Carol became responsible for getting themselves dressed, fed and on the bus. Their breakfast was always ready. If they missed the school bus, they'd have to walk and accept the resultant tardy slips. I wouldn't drive them to school, nor would I remind them of the time.

The school was too far away for such young children to reach on foot, but I was not to interfere in the natural results of their actions. Many a morning I heard them rough-housing until it was almost too late, but one or the other would suddenly remember the bus and they, luckily, always caught it.

What if they'd missed the bus? I'd follow them in the car to insure their safety but keep out of sight to insure the lesson's impact. But I prayed each morning they'd realize the time and journey to school the fast, safe way.

Years later, although their new high school was six miles away catching the bus was still their responsibility. The first time they had to walk, Carol returned home with blistered heels which we commiserated over and carefully doctored.

My neighbor scolded me for not taking John and Carol to school when I had an available car. I responded, if I built an airplane, I wouldn't be a successful builder unless my airplane flew. Rearing children meant helping them become independent of their parents – not dependent upon them. In the real world you pay for your own mistakes. My paying for my children's errors now wouldn't help them except in the short run. Besides, mistakes become rarer when you pay for your own. Where did I get the courage to buck "the norm"? You know where.

I cringed as a child when a mother would screech my playmate's name to bring her home from five doors away. There had to be a better way for our children. Prayer gave us our family's two-note whistle. Whenever the children heard me whistle our code, they came running, for it usually meant something good: lemonade when the weather was hot, a chance to play in the sprinklers, a trip to the park. On occasion it meant they'd dropped jackets or school books where they didn't belong, and I'd called them in to restore order. Sometimes it signaled a trip to the dentist. I kept a running tally of the perceived positives and negatives – keeping the sum decidedly positive.

Today if Cliff or I lose each other when shopping, the whistled code pinpoints our location. It also calls either of us into the house for a phone call or a meal.

My mother was creative in her discipline. She believed the unknown and unexpected to be more a detriment to misbehavior than the known could be. When my brother and I misbehaved, she suggested we go into the yard, pick a thin, wiry switch, strip off the leaves and bring it to her. It was a sobering activity. I don't recall her using the switch.

The switch which John and Carol repeatedly prepared for me was laid on the top of the refrigerator for immediate use the *next* time they misbehaved. By the next time it was too dry to be effective, so the activity was repeated. Our bushes became stripped of branches, but our children learned obedience without corporal punishment excepting a rare smack on the bottom from an open hand.

Twice negative behavior was checked in Carol, twice obedience was forced on John – my differing children. You know Who's love engineered the lessons.

One Sunday morning when Carol was almost three, she decided, "I won't," screamed out her anger and threw herself kicking onto the floor. This was our first tantrum – and our last.

I picked her up without a word, set her into the tub and turned on the cold water from the shower. Shock. She was calmly dried and redressed for church in play clothes since her starched dress and Mary Janes' were wet. Her damp hair was combed into a ponytail instead of Sunday's curls.

Carol was five when I first suspected she might be lying. My question had concerned brushing her teeth. Her, "Yes, I have." sounded guilty, but my quick check showed a damp toothbrush.

One Friday evening we changed to go as a family to the movies; "101 Dalmatians" was showing. Again Carol responded, "Yes," to the subject of tooth brushing, again the odd look, but this time her toothbrush was dry.

Cliff and John enjoyed the movie while Carol and I stayed home. I told her not brushing one's teeth wasn't a major catastrophe but "lying" was. Daddy and I had to be able to trust everything our children said in order to defend them from problems. A liar loses far more valuable opportunities than just missing a movie.

That evening she tried, unsuccessfully, to engage me in games or story-reading. She had to supply her own entertainment, for I wouldn't fill her thinking time.

Carol was an adult before "101 Dalmatians" was mentioned again. Missing the movie had made a *major* impression.

Cliff and I repeatedly reminded both children of our pride in their honesty and trustworthiness. To prove our trust, we let them babysit themselves when they reached eleven and twelve and we weren't far away.

One day John came home late from junior high. A substitute teacher had insisted he stay after class and pick up "spit-wads". She didn't believe him when he said he hadn't thrown them.

The next morning I handed John a letter for his teacher and suggested he read it before sealing the envelope. In the note I told the teacher I was happy John could be of assistance in cleaning the classroom, but she was in error in blaming him for the mess. I was certain he hadn't been at fault, because he had said so. *Our John doesn't lie.*

The only barrier between a child's negative potential and the law with its flashing lights appears to be parental authority. A child misbehaves in order to test his or her limits – to experience cause and effect. Parents hold firm to protect the child from his or her actions. But holding firm isn't easy, it requires the strength of God.

When John was twelve and refused to obey a house rule, I mentioned quietly, "If you're unhappy living with us, please find some place you can be happier. Choosing to live with us means obeying."

When he promptly decided he was man enough to go it alone, I suggested he pack a lunch; he might become hungry. John spent the day playing with neighborhood children; but when in late afternoon he walked in the front door, I walked him right back out, saying, "Only those who live in a house can walk in without knocking. You can't live with us unless you accept house rules."

That was the longest day Carol and I ever experienced. It was growing dark and cold. She was in tears, and I wanted desperately to hang a jacket on the line so he'd have something to keep away the chill, but I didn't. All I could do was pray for him somewhere outside and for Carol and me waiting inside. Before long he knocked and asked readmittance to family and its rules.

Only one other major clash of wills occur. John enjoyed solid-tone school shirts and looked good in them, but at the start of the eighth grade he chose plaid shirts instead. Not two weeks later, John said he hated his plaid shirts and wanted solid shirts to wear to school. His old shirts, out-grown, had been given to the church for the needy.

We bought John one new solid shirt to wear to church. We promised to replace his school shirts when worn-out or out-grown, but not before.

John breezed into breakfast one school morning in his Sunday shirt. I suggested he especially enjoy wearing it. When he asked, "Why?", I told him he'd never wear that shirt again. I'd either cut it up or give it away, but if he wore it to school it meant *the end* of his shirt. He exited for school, returned thirty seconds later, changed shirts in his room, and left with a stronger respect for parental authority.

Our children although they shared their father's Scandinavian coloring, are very different.

Before Carol was born, I had asked God to make her a "late bloomer" as was I. Precocious daughters scared me. He complied. As she grew I prayed repeatedly for the right opportunity to talk with her of "birds and bees." The time seemed very slow in coming, but the time He chose for our talk was special for two reasons.

I'd wanted to try sculpting but doors repeatedly closed whenever I checked classes and opportunities – until we moved to Denver. There an inner restriction was lifted. I could buy materials at an art store, but they didn't have the clay I sought. They only had a 10 x 15 x 1 inch sheet of dark wax. I bought the wax.

Like the goose which couldn't be cut or cooked, this wax was too hard to cut when cold, too sticky to handle when warm. I would have given up had I not been given my object to sculpt during a Sunday sermon. The text was Isaiah 6, the scripture began, "In the year that King Uzziah died...," and described a seraphim. Of course. Wings hid its face and feet; no one had ever seen one; a seraphim was a perfect subject for someone who didn't know how to sculpt.

I found a desk lamp heated the wax just enough to be malleable. Pieces could be added when needed or cut away when not needed. This was a perfect medium for an amateur.

While I sculpted this heavenly form, school let out and Carol joined me at the table. Our talk roamed far and wide. During this comfortable time, the words which I'd held in trust were received in comfort and love.

The funds for casting the seraphim in bronze became another miracle. So was its creation by this novice and its casting via the lost-wax method – when we'd been told this couldn't be done. The bronze seraphim sits today in our living room, a reminder of God's many gifts.

Whenever I asked God about sharing my faith with our children, the answer was "No." They belonged to Him; He would choose the time and place of their teaching. Could we not have a family prayer time? No, none other than mealtime grace. John and Carol were merely mine to enjoy. Yet they knew the motives, the conversations, the activities which fed me even though I couldn't describe them.

When Carol was in high school she enjoyed art, flying kites and riding her bike more than academics. She had many friends. One day Cliff and I remarked that the laughing carload of girls we had just deposited at school for an evening function were a decided mixture. Our girl had gathered a few misfits and a few socially elite. She was the catalyst by which they blended. Nice talent, that.

When John was a senior in high school, he and his friends decided to spend Easter week camping in the California mountains near Placerville. Their determination to take this trip was so strong they didn't mention or stop for several of God's warning roadblocks.

A narrow bridge crossing the river had become our favorite mountain spot. Cliff and the children often bounced rocks off the boulders below or watched their stones splash the surface of still pools. Here John took his friends. He and one buddy explored the stream bank while three others chucked rocks from above.

A rock went wild, straight for John. His best friend, who'd thrown the rock, screamed a warning. John turned at the scream and took the blow in his right eye.

Placerville is a tiny, sleepy town, but to Placerville a renowned eye surgeon had retired the previous month. He was registered with the local hospital and arrived shortly after John. Fine surgery saved our son's peripheral vision, but John lost all direct vision from his right eye.

Bandaged, John shushed my tears with the words, "God saved my life twice: once when the rock missed my temple, the second time because I'll never have to go to war. God must have something important for me to do."

The friend's insurance company was sure we'd sue. We didn't. We were deeply grateful John had received the rock and not thrown it. Costing a friend his sight would be far harder for John to bear than losing his own sight.

Our active son spent the next months flat on his back. His doctor took no risks, fearing John's other eye could be affected by the trauma. John studied with a home teacher and received his high school diploma by mail while classmates celebrated.

John soon returned to full activity. Not being an avid reader, he was less handicapped than others might be. His left iris is green, his right is black from a permanently dilated pupil – a rather dashing effect.

Our children joined us in snow skiing and swimming when five and six. Now barely forty, they still share scuba trips and ski vacations – especially when Cliff and I pick up the tab for them. We are amazingly good friends. I'd always expected to love my grown children but I'd never expected to like them this much.

John is a handsome, creative, hard-working mechanical engineer. He is still close to Cliff and me, however I'm constantly relearning my role is to pray for him, not to help him avoid mistakes. God has John on a steep learning curve following the breakup of his only marriage. Although it's painful, John sees God's hand in it and seeks His will. We are grateful.

Cliff's mother, Grammy, was the communicator who honored birthdays and anniversaries for her generation. I have for mine. Now when flowers arrive on Mother's Day, I'm amazed our son and daughter capably carry the torch for the younger generation.

Carol and I are closer than we've ever been in our lives. She's supportive, loving and capable, very like Cliff in being truly nice to be around. Years ago she recognized our difference and how glad she was not to be me. I'm glad, too, for she has much to give of which

I'm not capable. As a hospital occupational therapist Carol works with stroke patients. She's fresh, real and active – the beautiful California woman of today.

Carol shares a home with a dear friend. Neither marriage nor children appear in their future, but they're grounded in faith and happy together.

A psychologist and I once talked informally of children when I told her Carol was ten before her bonds to John broke and the wall between us liftedThe psychologist asked a strange question, "How did *you* change then?" I told her I'd surrendered my many "have-tos" and accepted in their place "want-tos".

"Of course," she murmured.

8

Flying Carpets

Books have carried me to distant cities or stars, deep into minutia, backwards and forwards in time. They have introduced me to wonderful people, real and imaginary, and shown how others look and speak and act. They have taught thousands of subjects, shallowly or in depth; refreshed with their charm or humor; startled with their observations. I love the printed word.

Once an indiscriminate reader, I now found books to be chosen for me, the time-passers as well as the masterpieces. And exact answers or verifications appear in my reading when I seem most to need them.

Occult and horror books and films have long been forbidden.

My Inner Guidance supplies an alarm system. It's as though I hear bells when truth rings out, a buzzer when something which seems true isn't.

But now isn't time for "Who's your favorite author?" It's time to share the truths God has sent through the writings of other "Mousehole" travelers. Most have stood the test of time. I'll share the ideas I found significant in hopes you also may find them so.

The Holy Bible holds words of unmatched truth which return in memory to verify the road I travel. Although it's no longer allowed as my map or daily companion, it has supplied the core of my knowledge about God. Previously memorized scriptures have become real with experience. And, to my wonder, the road I travel has never contradicted its teaching – even though it sometimes seems to.

The Christian's Secret of a Happy Life, Hannah Whitall Smith, Word Publishers, 1883, was the gift of a Christian in Ohio. I had read only through the second chapter before closing the book and following the blueprint this Quaker author suggested nearly 100 years earlier. God's word through her showed me the way to Him – through my will, not my emotions. This book triggered my being born anew.

I reread and mulled each chapter before moving to the next. It took two months to absorb her words even though the material wasn't difficult and truly fascinated me.

Surely all I need do is place this miraculous book in the hands of those I love and each will join me in the Kingdom, I thought. I've given away more copies than I can count, but the desired results didn't happen. Recipients weren't at my place of need – weren't sufficiently flattened. But I'm reassured with the thought one never knows when a planted seed will sprout.

The Road Less Traveled, M. Scott Peck, M.D., Touchstone Press of Simon & Schuster, Inc, 1978, is the book which I've given in quantity more recently. God's loving voice speaks here of the pain of problem-solving, the hiding places we choose to escape the light of truth. Peck's troubled people, troubled relationships, are the people I know. His language is fresh – solution is spiritual growth.

Psychologist Peck gives a memorable analogy of marriage. He likens marriage to the climbers' base camp. More time must be spent in making the camp than in climbing the peaks or the expedition fails. The camp must supply rest and nourishment, so climbers can face their challenge renewed. Without an adequate camp, they fail to reach goals or fall in the striving.

I, as most women, have been the primary keeper of the marriage. Cliff assisted, but earning our living was his primary job. With retirement he's assuming ever larger responsibilities in base-camp-keeping while I'm freer to climb mountains.

Power In Praise, Merlin R. Carothers, Foundation of Praise, Box 2518, Escondidio, CA, 1972, is especially helpful to those caught in impos-sible circumstances. Chaplain Carothers shares numerous miracles which come through the application of this one Biblical truth: **all things work together for good...in everything give thanks...count it all joy.** Praise God for a brother dying with cancer? Praise God for an alcoholic husband? Oh, yes!

The Hiding Place, Corrie ten Boom, Bantam Books, 1971, also shares how God's miracles change hideous circumstances. She, a 50-year-old Dutch heroine of the anti-Nazi underground, tells of the terrible fleas in the concentration camp into which she and her sister were thrust. Why did God allow the fleas? Weren't their lives hellish enough?

But shortly Corrie and her fellow inmates, packed tightly into a too-small barrack, praised God and thanked Him for the fleas. They alone could share a smuggled-in Bible, quietly pray, study and worship. Guards, who kept all other prisoners under close surveillance, would have punished them for such behavior but stayed away from Corrie's barracks to escape being bitten.

Mere Christianity, C. S. Lewis, Macmillan Company, 1943, offered me new understanding of this life. One chapter shines like a beacon in my memory. It's entitled, 'The Great Sin.' Lewis builds an impressive argument that "pride" is the complete anti-God state of mind--the greatest sin.

This Cambridge professor died in 1963, leaving a rich Christian legacy of fiction and nonfiction. His seven Narnia books for children show Christianity through fantasy. Three Perelandra books show it through science fiction. *The Great Divorce* portrays heaven and hell.

His slimmest volume, *Screwtape Letters & Screwtape Proposes a Toast* presents a humorous, devil's view of the world. One scene remains vivid...a senior devil counsels his nephew, an apprentice devil, "To gain a human's soul you must be careful of one thing, your human must never have fun. All fun comes from the enemy above."

The Release of the Spirit and *The Normal Christian Life*, Watchman Nee, More, P.O. Box 18505, Indianapolis, IN 46218, 1965, gave me new framework for housing my Christianity. This prolific Chinese author's writings ceased after his imprisonment in 1952, but his insights will never die.

The Twelve Steps: A Spiritual Journey, Recovery Publications, Inc. 1988, is a book I currently read with others as a member of a Sunday School class. This book outlines the steps God uses to awaken me and others from our dysfunctional lives and lead us into Himself. Most in our class have come from abusing childhoods or addictions and some even from prison. We know our very lives depend upon our walking with God. We love each other; everyone is honest and real, sharing pain, hesitant steps, or surprise at this new way of act-ing and reacting. I wish everyone could be involved with a 12-step program, for everyone has need of it.

I Will Lift Up Mine Eyes, Glenn Clark, Harper & Row, 1937, was a flawed book, warning bells sounded when I read of ladders and rules. But it was a glorious book, too. It held two special gifts. 'The Hinds Feet that Lead to High Places' section made me understand afresh how God is inte-grating my will, mind and emotions.

'The Soul's Sincere Desire' concept hurried God's work in me. Upon reading that God had placed His desires in each of us, I determined to find out what he had planned for me. Apparently I was to sit with pad and pen and look deeply within myself to see what I truly desire. Discoveries were to be recorded. Those desires hurtful to others and those for which I was unwilling to expend effort should be deleted. Those which appeared material, a car or a career, should be retained. Lastly, I was to give back to God my desires and let Him fulfill them in His time and way.

Three desires appeared from deep within me and were written on my pad. The first warmed me, the second didn't surprise me, the third was a shocker.

My first desire was that Cliff and the children should find a faith such as mine. My second desire was to travel. My third desire was to be slim and chic. "Whoa. Where did this come from? It can't be from you, Lord, can it?"

"Can this, your third desire, be struck from your list for any of the given reasons?"

"No, Lord, but pursuit of beauty seems so trivial, so unbecoming in a Christian. Surely you don't mean this for me. I long ago accepted being a dumpy, middle-aged home economics teacher."

"Leave it on your list, my child. Your body is my temple and worthy of love even as is your soul. Leave this to me."

I closed my pad and my eyes, thanked God and gave Him back His three "desires". I never again prayed for the two desires I still deemed less worthy.

Although one never knows where another resides spiritually, it appears Cliff and the children's faith now parallels mine. My first desire has been fulfilled.

Since then we have lived and traveled extensively in Europe and the United States. Scuba diving and underwater photography has taken us to exotic locales in Micronesia, Australia, Borneo, the Indian Ocean, the Caribbean, the Philippians...even supplying a side trip to Hong Kong and China. Consulting and speaking fly me to major cities. My desire to travel is constantly fulfilled.

Am I slim and chic? Not in those words, but my desire has been fulfilled. I enjoy looking as I do. And the books I have written, the business which God formed for me, and the healing He's done in others through me have all been built upon my desire. Are you curious how this came about? Good. I'll answer as many of your questions as possible in a later chapter.

9

The Front Line

One evening a couple with some fame in Christian circles spoke at our church. They told of miracles which had happened to them a number of years before, reminiscing as do old soldiers over their "war". The same words had apparently been spoken so often they were dry, the juices gone. One couldn't doubt their experiences, but I left saddened because the spiritual vitality which had filled them then was only a memory now. I, too, have my war stories, but unlike the famous couple, my voice has been quiet until now. Will my narrative, too, be dead? Not knowing the answer, I trust God for living words and go back in memory.

Prayer Groups hadn't appealed to me before our time in Ohio. I'd considered them for old ladies. But when we arrived there my strength was so low, my faith so dead I asked the church caller what her church offered for spiritual growth. When she mentioned Prayer Groups, I thought, "No way, I'm not *that* bad off."

During our second week in a Sunday School class, an attractive dentist's wife mentioned something they'd discussed in their Prayer Group. She wasn't old or dull, she was sharp, and the subject she mentioned interested me. That afternoon I called Ginnie and asked when her Group met and could I join them.

The Prayer Group I joined was composed of five personable women in their thirties. Although well-educated and dedicated, they had a Group which was limping, strangling for lack of honesty. Its members carefully monitored their words for this was a small town.

I, who'd be there only a few months and had nothing to lose, was for the first time free to speak out without fear of consequences. I did, and to my amazement was loved even though my imperfections became totally visible.

The Group revived, as did I. And Ginnie became a bosom friend and Christian sister. God's love through her supported me so safely I dared trust Him with my life.

She gave me Hannah Smith's book as well as Oswald Chambers' *My Utmost For His Highest*, a daily devotional written in 1935 which I still keep by my bedside and read almost daily

A Prayer Group was the first thing I sought when we returned to California, for I needed friends with whom to share the wonder and discoveries of my new life. During those short years I can't recall any accomplishments of mine. But one lesson and three beautiful gifts were given me – two of the gifts through the same dear Prayer Group friend. First the lesson. Carrie, a friendly, Switzerland-educated blond from South America looked so fun-loving I tried to maneuver myself into sitting next to her at a church luncheon. To my disappointment, my seat mate was, instead, Maria, a quiet, dark skinned, woman with a heavy accent.

Well all's not lost. Carrie's leaving her chair to come speak to me before the activities begin, I thought. Not so. Carrie came over to speak with Maria. Maria, it turns out, is a sensitive, brilliant South American who speaks five languages. Jane is a bigot who speaks only English.

Shame still stains my face when I remember my smugness, but God forgave me, and Maria and Carrie became close, equally loved, Prayer Group sisters.

Enid, a fellow alto, asked one choir rehearsal night if I'd care to ride with her that week. She was exercising the neighbor's horses. Yes!!! I'd loved riding as a child but hadn't ridden for years. Twice a week all spring Enid and I rode the trails of Palos Verde. And when summer came, she had gentled two extra horses so John and Carol could join us. We groomed and saddled our mounts, rode the trails in glee, practiced drills in a hillside ring, watered, fed and brushed our trusty steeds, and gathered duck eggs in the grass by the tack room. Pure heaven. I'll never forget the wondrous summer God gave us through Enid.

Two special gifts came through Muriel, an artist in our California Prayer Group.

The first was an introduction to canoeing. Twice our family joined theirs on day trips with three canoes. What lively days, paddling down the Russian River or out to the San Pedro breakwater with bursts of song, shouts of laughter, even picnic stops with guitar and watermelon.

As we left Los Angeles for a new assignment in Denver, Muriel gave me a choice of all her prints. She also told me I had inspired a picture she'd be printing and sending to me in our new home.

Muriel works in silk screen and block print. The glowing print she sent us was 24 x 36 inches, numbered 3/10, and entitled, "Lit and Unlit."

The print shows two contrasting figures. On the lower left is a squat male figure dressed as one of the British "pearlies", buttons sewn all over his clothing and cap. He holds a tiny cross in one hand and from his body protrude electric plugs. He's block-printed black – obviously unlit – yet trying to reflect faith or to get plugged-in.

The major figure is a glowing presence with arms extended, roots reaching downward, hair radiating light. In its center both pumping heart and percolating coffee pot are distinguishable. The colors, sunny yellow, tomato red, lime green and a touch of sky blue are bright with energy. This glorious print obviously hangs in honor in our home. But it's a humbling picture, for alone I'm "Unlit." Only when His love shines through me do I appear "Lit."

The Denver Prayer Group began when I couldn't find one and so invited my neighbor, an Episcopal priest's wife, to join me for coffee and talk on Thursday morning. The next week we each asked someone else, and in a few months our family room was full from nine till four every Thursday. Months later another neighbor opened her home and the Prayer Group continued with a seven to eleven evening session.

There was no leader, no lesson, no officers, no schedule, no dues, no formal prayer. Coffee I could serve weekly for years without resentment, so coffee was all I served. Anyone who needed nourishment or a change of beverage brought their own.

We had only one male in our daytime group, a radio announcer who worked nights. His wife came during her lunch hour and attended the evening sessions.

Known religious affiliations included Catholic, Baptist, Mormon, Church of Christ, Presbyterian, Episcopal, and Agnostic, but there could have been others.

Churches were sometimes prayed for, but doctrines were never discussed.

Honesty was an unspoken by-law. The sharing of hopes, fears, concerns, and answers to prayer bound us into a family for whom Christ was the head. Miracles flourished.

One of our daytime members, Sally, had a daughter who required continuing medical attention. Family resources became exhausted, Sally was unskilled and their several children made her working seem impossible. She shared her financial concern with the PG.

As was customary, anyone who had a solution offered it, and PG members, relying on His corporate truth, screened the possibilities.

One member suggested Sally have her husband determine exactly how much total salary he *needed* to keep their heads up, to write that amount on a slip of paper, fold it, and put the paper away – petitioning only God for the extra income. PG members concurred in believing Sally's family should trust God to supply the additional funds.

The next week Sally said her husband had wryly followed the suggestion. How could it hurt? The amount he wrote on the paper wasn't rounded off to the nearest ten. It was exactly the amount needed monthly, an unusual number. The next morning at work his boss asked him to stop by the office. When he did, the boss flipped him a slip of paper with an amount written on it. *The numbers exactly matched those he'd written the night before.* This was his new salary, pro-rated to the first of the month. It was more than the company normally gave, in an increment which they never offered, at a time when a salary review was most unlikely. We all thanked God for this miracle.

At a neighbor's coffee, my hostess, Jo, mentioned a novel she'd enjoyed. The same day at the grocery store Jo's novel seemed to leap into my cart. I soon discovered her novel was written by a Christian, and further realized Jo must be invited to the PG.

Months later, Jo said she came that first Thursday to set a group of simple women straight in their theology. She had studied a number of faiths intensely and felt highly competent. She found, to her surprise, theology wasn't mentioned, the room radiated love, and hearts and emotions were shared – not head knowledge.

The week before Jo's third meeting with the PG, I was reading a Christian book which fascinated me. Suddenly, I was told, "Give that book to Jo right now."

"Can't I just finish it first?", I asked, "I read very fast."

The answer was, "No," so I was panting when I handed the book to Jo. A quick explanation of why I brought it, plus a request to have it back when she'd finished reading it, and I returned home.

Jo looked ten years younger when she came early to the next PG. She was relaxed and smiling. When the group had gathered, she shared her big news. She'd taken the book I'd lent her into the bathroom to read in the tub – one of her favorite pastimes. She'd read only a portion of it before feeling God's presence. He told her how long He'd waited for her to stop trying to earn her salvation. He wanted to gift her with it. She accepted His gift, and to her surprise, the cigarettes which she'd tried for years to quit, had no further appeal. She'd long believed if she could just quit smoking God would love her. When she allowed God to love her, the desire to smoke was gone. Jo and her beautiful husband became hosts to the evening PG.

My days became filled with praise, thanks giving and activity. Our minister even began sending those he couldn't reach to me for counseling. I was present when bodies, minds and spirits became healed. I truly believed God had chosen this format as my lifetime ministry, but I was mistaken. It was only my "war." Whenever a pattern begins to develop in my walk of faith, God moves me to another arena.

10

A New Language

For a time letters tied me to my Prayer Group family. One letter of mine to a PG member was several pages long, but as I sealed the envelope I couldn't recall the topic on which I'd written. Should I reread it? No. I sealed the envelope and left my desk to post it in the mailbox on the street. As I strolled out the door, divine laughter rumbled in me. I'd pleased Him in some way, I supposed, delighting in His sense of humor. His love so engulfed me I didn't mind not being "in" on the joke.

A week later I received a phone call from the person to whom I'd written. She thanked me profusely, for that very morning she'd had a problem arise which she took to God. Giving Him her problem gave her peace but not a solution. The solution, my letter, arrived in her mailbox the same morning. The nature of her problem I never learned.

Days seemed long. They would have been peaceful had I not wanted so much to *do* for God. He wanted me to *be* for Him. I must relearn again to take one moment at a time, trusting Him to keep me on-track. "Please, Lord, at least tell me WHY you've removed me from active service, from counseling, from Christian friends, from Christian groups," I prayed.

"My dear child, you haven't been demoted. You've been promoted into a different kind of class. Before, my love through others was part of your sustenance; now, you must feed directly from me. Besides, I've separated you from your groups in order for you to learn a new language, a language free of 'God talk'. The ministry I give you will reach those who'd never listen to you with your present word choice. Trust me; submit to my forging. You will become the tool which I require."

We did receive a visit from a large, rough woman whom I'd counseled in Denver. Never would I have chosen her as a friend, but she was chosen for me as a Christian sister. What an incongruous pair we made as we laughingly explored San Francisco, arm-in-arm. She was dressed as though a lumberjack; I was slimmer, more chic, than I'd ever been in my life.

Yes, my desire to be slim and chic was coming true. An excellent diagnostician taught me how to control my edema, excessive water retention. On his regime I lost seventeen pounds in two months.

Further, an attractive woman came to buy our freezer and has remained a lifelong friend. She looked wonderful, yet she had no better face or figure than I. Upon probing, I found she had taken an excellent image seminar and thus knew the kinds of clothing and accessories, the makeup and hairstyle which best emphasized her uniqueness. I wanted such information for both Carol and myself so we, also, took the course. Not long after, Cliff had his colors done. John had to be blackmailed into going, but we became a family of attractive, color-coordinated individuals.

Old PG friends didn't understand this new interest. They agreed I'd left God, saw me shooting off-target. Whenever I checked within, however, I was told my body was God's temple and I hadn't left him – I was doing exactly what he'd set for me. He wanted my appearance healed not just my spirit and emotions.

Although speaking of my faith to my new friends was blocked, I could speak to them of image consulting – of their untapped beauty. And I saw the healing that improved appearance promoted in these men and women.

Psychiatrists say healed psyches produce improved appearance. I found improved appearance heals psyches.

The theory which came with my colors forced me to explore my self concept. Feminine colors hardly belonged on a woman wearing white cotton panties. My lingerie changed to nude-tone and silky. And although the steps felt painful, my femininity was at last accepted by me and reinforced by others.

Slowly I realized I'd return to work when the children left for college. I wanted to even though my income wasn't needed. Yes, it was God's will. No, He wouldn't tell me what I'd be doing. Rats!

While doing research for Mr. Don, the color analyst to whom I'd brought my friends, I asked how he'd ever found a job which so completely suited him. He said he'd been unhappy as a commercial artist but didn't know why until he'd had his 'innate abilities' tested by the nonprofit Johnson O'Connor Research Foundation in Los Angeles. (They now have centers in most major cities.) He was told he needed to spend 90% of his time with people instead of the current 10%. He needed to teach and analyze with his art. Johnson O'Connor's collection of aptitudes of successful people from all occupations pinpoint the strengths and weaknesses necessary to each occupation.

We made appointments for four with Johnson O'Connor's center and our family took a trip to Los Angeles. Cliff wanted insurance against being promoted into an area where he'd be incompetent. John wanted verification that mechanical engineering was his best major in college. Carol didn't think she was college material but needed direction. I, the most eager, wanted to know where I should direct my talent and skills.

The tests, usually given over four half-days, had been compressed into two solid days at our request. Spreading them would be worth the extra hotel time, we realized afterward. I was so tired by the end of the second day my mind glitched – I missed hearing one musical note, had to guess on the answer.

These tests were more similar to mechanical, intellectual, musical puzzles than language-based. Most were administered one-on-one. Several were grouped via sight or sound. Results fascinated us.

Cliff worked well with people, but he must keep engineering a part of his life since unused aptitudes reduce both pleasure and output. When Cliff later was transferred into personnel, we built a house to use his mechanical abilities.

John and Carol were encouraged to choose small colleges where teacher/pupil ratios remained low. Both are slow readers and handle paperwork poorly. Our counselor suggested they tell each teacher at the beginning of the semester they'll do poorly on tests and on written papers. But since these can't accurately measure their interest or knowledge, can they do extra projects to show their facility and increase their grades?

Mechanical engineering was perfect for John. Carol's best choices included heavy equipment operator or occupational therapist. Her high aptitudes had been counter-balanced by lows, thus her poor school grades. When we queried about her completing college, we heard, "No problem." She tests extremely high in determination. This girl can do anything she sets out to do.

I tested virtually unemployable. Too-many high aptitudes means no job has enough breadth. They suggested my solving big problems – urban redevelopment or feeding the world – not realizing my impatience with long projects.

For several months I thrashed around, undirected, either my Inner Guidance was stilled or I couldn't or didn't listen. Should I go back to college? Take what?

Queries took me to the California Department of Education – home economics division. I asked the highest authority I could reach "What's important enough to keep me in the home economics field? I enjoy classroom teaching of both children and adults, but don't want to repeat areas I've already experienced."

My authority, a natural catalyst, mentioned at least twenty nontraditional possibilities. Teaching on television "stuck." It felt right. Its entrepreneurial nature would also supply the flexibility my aptitudes required.

My first taste of television was doing free, taped "do bits" for a news program in Sacramento. The program director was my neighbor's brother. Response was encouraging; but I'd have quit if "my caring for the audience" hadn't shown in my face and manner.

At this time I also served as unpaid consultant to a black committee for East Bay urban renewal. We were remodeling a house for use as a classroom. I was the only white. God protected me when I drove alone at night into the ghetto. A grin from me always brought a grinning response from strangers on the streets.

There I learned the desperate need of the under-privileged for practical and fiscal role models. They see the lives of the wealthy on television, the lives of the destitute in their neighborhoods. Totally absent was the middle-class practicality and thrift which could spring them from their prisons – practicality which we take for granted.

I soon realized I wanted to do a daily half-hour show in a modest, one-room apartment. "Living well on less" would demonstrate decorating the apartment, enter-taining, cooking, keeping a checkbook and balancing a budget. It was needed; it could even be practical, for sponsors would have virtually half-hour commercials. Someone's equipment and supplies would appear regu-larly on camera. But wanting to do it and doing it are different.

But, again through a friend, I landed an on-camera teaching position on a thirty-minute public-service pro-gram at one of San Francisco's major stations. It aired daily at six am. Each Friday I brought everything needed, including graphics and four changes of clothes, to their studio. Each show found me alone on camera for nearly 29 minutes with no breaks, no retakes. We taped five shows back-to-back. I did four series, 55 shows in all, within a six month period.

My beginning salary was only fifteen dollars a show, plus expenses, but the educational benefits were enormous. Each morning I could see which colors "flared" the camera, how certain motions seemed ugly or awkward, how a word choice or phrase made me cringe. I learned and improved.

When the "pilot" of my daily consumer show, promised by the station, was denied since there was nothing on paper, Cliff and I financed a pilot at an independent facility. The show couldn't be aired, due to technical failings, but it captured the essence of the idea.

Cliff was reassigned to Houston; and although I showed the pilot, no one bought it or me. I appeared on all the talk shows with "do bits" to become known to a new audience, and spoke to groups at every opportunity.

Meanwhile, Houston's PBS station hired me to pilot my series. The pilot was taped with a flawless twenty-five minute demonstration captured on the first attempt. But when the short interview segment was obviously flawed, they refused to retake it – even though we remained miked and eager to redo. The pilot, apparently scrapped by management before the taping, never appeared. My producer later told me management felt no one would believe one woman could successfully sew, cook, design interiors and handle money.

They apparently forgot women have spent generations being expert at everything. We've had to be.

Apparently this project deserved one more try. Cliff and I hired a producer and set-designer and leased Houston's NBC station long enough to tape two half-hour pilots. We called the show, PIONEERING THE PRESENT, and it almost flew. I took the pilots coast-to-coast to advertising agencies and public relations heads of major companies. I listed the benefits they'd realize from covering the production costs of this "barter" show. That summer, "barter" shows ceased being "hot," and the two sponsors who verbally bought the show backed out.

An unsold pilot is comparable to a dry well in oil drilling. We had an empty hole into which we'd poured many dollars, and I'd poured six years.

Cliff had never believed the show would go, but had financed it for me. He was sorry for me when it failed but took comfort in seeing his judgment vindicated. I was given to see this project as education. Going back for a doctorate would take a similar investment in time and money but it wouldn't have taught the lessons learned from this project. This failed attempt wasn't a detour even though it seemed to be.

The pilot gained me a consultant's job with J.C. Penneys, Houston Division. I sold their advertising director the benefits of my representing them on radio and television. As Penney's Home Economist, I chose the topics, set up the bookings, and billed Penney's by the show. For four years I appeared on local talk shows, bringing how-tos to viewers and listeners, using Penney's products to illustrate my points. The company had no position for consultants doing media, may still not, but I built goodwill for them and confidence and skill in their customers.

Meanwhile my speaking topic, "Enhancing Personal Beauty," became popular and was expanded into a six-hour seminar. Mr. Don came regularly to Houston to give my students and clients their colors. When he could no longer come, I stopped giving seminars and began a project which badly frightened me.

For some time God had been closing doors and directing me toward writing a text to accompany my classes. Since no texts existed, a large part of seminar fees had been spent for duplication of materials.

I'd never even written an article. Letters had been okay – they weren't long – but a book? I'd grow to my chair. "Please don't make me do a book," I pleaded with Him.

"Silly child, you forget you can lean on me for every word. I'd not ask this of you if I wasn't prepared to supply you. Trust me."

Four chapters were written, rewritten and rewritten again the first year. The second year only one chapter went into the folder. The chapter in this book entitled, "Grammy," will explain why. The third year the words flowed from fingertips through typewriter onto page as fast as I could type – as though I read a fascinating novel.

Whenever I would ask when, how, I could acknowledge Him as author, I was told to wait. The last page referred to Him gently. But readers have written me they knew His voice from the first word.

Look Like Yourself & Love It!, *The 4-T Guide To Personal Style*, Triad Press, 1980, was in my arms in the fall of 1980. I cried all the way home from the bindery and for months afterwards felt humbled by this gift of God's. Even today, when I autograph a copy of this book He wrote through me, I'm awed by His love...both to me and to those who read the book.

God gave me a Texas corporation in 1974 which I named after Him, Triad Interests, Inc., for the Trinity. The final pilots carried its name. We called the division under which we published my first book, Triad Press. My first title has sold more than 12,000 copies and a number of universities still use it as an image text. But the planned promotion for this book never materialized; *Look Like Yourself & Love It!* never entered the bookstores. Cliff was transferred to Holland a few months after its publication date and I, being in God's pocket the day Cliff called about our going overseas said, "Yes. Since He wrote it, He can handle the sales."

God supplied the tools and insight whereby Tri-D Consultants, another Triad Interests division, has trained more than sixty image consultants who have worked in seven countries. We supply them and other consultants with books, cassettes, supplies and makeup. Our research in personal appearance enhancement appears to be foremost in the industry.

The tools we developed to train our consultants led to an expanded image concept, and it took just over a year for Him to turn this new body of material into my second book, *Style Strategy: Winning the Appearance Game*, Triad Press, 1988.

The image (personal appearance) industry must be very important to God, for He had me join each fledgling image association which tried to develop in the early days. We obviously needed one strong organization but I didn't know then which one would prosper. When the East Coast's AFIC joined the West coast's AIC, I knew where my energies belonged. I became the first VP-Marketing of AICI, the Association of Image Consultants International. I also served as AICI International Regional Advisor from '93-'95.

In 1993 I received our industry's highest award, an IMMIE for Dedication. What astonished me was this didn't come because I'd written the *AICI Member's Manual* and spent thousands of hours in developing association materials. It came because I was open to my colleagues – being a mentor. Isn't God wonderful? The old Jane had no time for anyone.

This book was written in only five weeks in 1988, although final edit and publishing didn't occur until 1996. Needless to say, I didn't want to write so personal a book. Could it be fair to my husband and children? But when God has a project in mind, who can tell Him, "No"? I've left Cliff, John and Carol in His hands once again.

It appears my fourth book won't be completed even though I've a patented multi-ethnic makeup selection and marketing system, plus notes on a new book on makeup application. Research and development is so satisfying; as is writing when God supplies the words.

Is Triad Interests, Inc. wildly successful? Yes, in satisfaction; no, financially. Cliff took over fulfillment, financial, inventory and photographic duties when he retired. Neither of us have ever taken a salary from the company; we still underwrite major expenses from family accounts. Funds invested in pilots have yet to be replaced in the family coffer.

Why continue? Personal returns are so great. Clients with crippled egos come to a consultant with skills similar to mine and leave standing tall, proud of the person God made them to be. Career men and women come for the appearance tools which bring promotions and confidence. Image consultants come for a fine-tuning of their appearance which brings new clients, new opportunities and for the materials which increase their incomes.

What of the future? It's hopeful. God has promised success, but I don't know whether that means a Jane who is being made whole or a financial return for the technology our company has developed. My current assignment is to develop the vocabulary and knowledge to market our cosmetic licensing program.

When our projects materialize, women will be saved time and money, gain promotions and respect and gain pride in the bodies and faces which God has given them. Our paradigm shift will aid manufacturers and retailers to minimize investment and maximize earnings while reducing waste. Are manufacturers listening? "Not yet." Will they listen? Perhaps, in God's time.

11

The Giver – The Taker

Lace, fragrance and femininity might surround other women, but not Lyda. As the eldest of five children she was born in the South to a Christian family. Her father bought small, general stores. He stocked and built clientele before selling at a profit and moving his family to another town, another store. In 1917 he moved his family to the fertile San Joaquin valley of California. There, in 1918, he lost his wife to cancer. Lyda was just eighteen, her youngest sister twelve.

What option had she? Someone had to "mother" the grieving household. She was the obvious choice. Besides, her dream of becoming a concert pianist had been recently smashed. She finally realized what others had hinted at, determination can't substitute for talent.

Her next seven years were spent in household management and sibling rearing with time out for a business course in accounting. Lyda knew she'd never marry – her father would always need her at home – but she wanted the financial and social independence supplied by outside employment.

Perched on the top of a tall accountant's stool this tiny, scrubbed-faced, dark-haired woman interested the tall trainee just hired by the utility company. But she refused his invitations, and he was soon transferred to Los Angeles.

Since one of Lyda's sisters worked in Los Angeles and repeatedly encouraged her to visit, Lyda decided to spend her vacation there. During her visit she accidently met again the tall man who'd intrigued her at work. His name was Frank.

How could it hurt if she had dinner with him her last night? They'd never see each other again, she rationalized. Frank's invitation was accepted.

The restaurant, overlooking the city, was reached by a long flight of stairs. The glittering view made it worth the climb. During their descent after a memorable dinner, Frank returned for her forgotten purse. Lyda, star-gazing, lost her balance and fell down the stairs.

Pain...ambulance siren...pain...white-gowned attendants...pain. Lyda awoke in a hospital bed unable to move her lower limbs. Her body was immobilized by sandbags. Besides massive bruising, she had broken her pelvis and would have to lie unmoving for six weeks.

Beside her bed was a large bouquet with a card from Frank saying he'd see her every evening she was in the hospital. He did.

Lyda slowly realized her father could manage without her. Wasn't he having to? She also realized she loved the tall, faithful man who made visiting hours fly past. She left the hospital with an engagement ring, finished her recuperation at home and was married there. She was twenty-six. Frank was thirty-two. The year was 1926.

One of eleven children from a poor farm in the South, Frank had left home in his teens to work as a railroad telegrapher. Baseball, hunting and fishing became passions. He settled in Kansas and might still be there had World War I not interrupted.

The Army Signal Corp transported him to California, but the war ended before he could be sent overseas. He loved the Golden State and remained.

Frank was selling utility stock when he and Lyda married. They built a new home, spent two months on a delayed honeymoon in Europe and started their family. The stock market was performing spectacularly and they thrilled to the ride – until it ended.

The Great Depression caught them with a small son, a daughter on the way, a house valued less than its mortgage, their furniture, car and clothes. Frank's lucrative job was gone, of course. The only position his company had available was one of "meter reader" in Long Beach, 45 miles away. Salary was $100 a month, but he took it.

After their daughter was born, they leased their Los Angeles home and moved into a Long Beach rental. His murderous commute was at last over.

In 1933 Long Beach was hit by a major earthquake. Frank, Lyda and the children escaped with their lives but lost everything breakable. Gone were the china and crystal – last ties to gracious living.

Frugality was for a time a necessity, but it became a lifestyle. Lyda and Frank carefully husbanded funds, food, clothing, equipment. Nothing was wasted.

Frank moonlighted by buying, rebuilding and selling used machinery and equipment. She canned produce, tended a garden in their backyard and remodeled hand-me-downs for her family. In the years following, she added household maintenance, bookkeeping, "rewinding" burned-out motors, "fletching" arrows for archery and making bow strings.

Frank said he'd been a bachelor too long to ever eat out again. So he didn't. He came home for lunch every day for fifty years.

Lyda soon realized Frank cared little for music, beauty or orderly surroundings. He worked on projects wherever there was space. It hurt her to surrender cleanliness and order, but Frank stood ten-feet-tall in her eyes, so she decided she'd want whatever he wanted.

Frank enjoyed the outdoors, hunting and fishing, and didn't care what food he ate as long as it didn't include tomatoes. Lyda cooked over camp fires, pulled her end of a cross-cut saw in the Oregon forests – cutting yew wood for bow staves, joined him in fishing and archery,

The "flapper era" of boyish figures had ruined her full breasts which didn't stay beautiful after binding. Her total involvement in Frank's world left her no time for being a woman. Her skin weathered, figure spread and hands roughened.

Lyda's cooking was uncreative, her housekeeping minuscule except for laundry. She never made time to play the piano or read, her earlier pleasures.

But she took time for prayer and Bible reading, and she insisted upon attending and giving to the church. Frank would never have attended had she not taken the children for years without him. Frank was baptized at the same time as their two children and said the table grace, but she remained the family's conscience.

Lyda flew to the aid of neighbors, friends, family. Nothing was too much to ask of her. She willingly gave her time and possessions. Their money belonged to Frank, she felt, so her sharing took other forms.

She was a superb and creative mother. She expected much from her children and loved them much. Joys increased and disappointments lessened when shared with her. She knew her children would never lie, never steal, never disappoint her. How could they after that?

Frank was the "star" of the family, the one who drew friends, told wonderful stories, was the center of activity. He could out-work, out-walk, out-shoot, out-fish other men. He was masculine and authoritative. His children fought over who would sit beside him at church.

Lyda and Frank gave their children the legacies of proper grammar, respect for authority, desire for education and willingness to work. But their greatest gift was the surety that nothing the children could ever do was bad enough to cost them their parent's love. Such unconditional love mirrors God's love. It's freeing, supporting and makes everything possible.

When I was young, I thought Lyda, my mother, was the most perfect Christian I had ever seen. She was totally giving, totally selfless. Her husband, the head of the house, loved and respected her. Bright, warm, sensitive and caring, could any woman be more Christian?

As I grew older, I watched her give away loved gifts she'd received for Christmas – as though others held more value than she. She refused to ask Daddy for things she really wanted, for they weren't worth risking a skirmish. She was, she said, saving all her ammunition for a really important fight.

Although she handled the checkbook and prepared the income tax, she wouldn't buy something she needed without first asking Daddy for the money. He released a minimum amount when she could justify the expenditure.

She waited years for a social security check of her own, wanting discretionary funds in order to give more to the church, to others, to buy things for herself. To her horror, her first and all subsequent social security payments didn't appear in her name; they were added to Daddy's check and thus became his. "No, I won't mention it to Daddy," she said. "And don't you mention it either. It's not worth it."

How does a "giver who refuses to take" affect her spouse? She teaches him to "take and never give." Her refusal to communicate her needs made him appear insensitive to them. Her unnecessary martyrdom was costly. It left them both only half the person God meant them to be.

For fifteen years I had blindly followed Mother's path in my marriage to Cliff. Thank God He lifted me away from it and set me down upon new, untracked turf.

How did they react to the new Jane? Uncomfortably. They felt they'd lost a dutiful daughter, and they had. Finding themselves displaced by God as my advisors, plus having to relate as adult to adult, instead of adult to child, stressed them. That they'd gained a loving daughter wasn't appreciated for some time.

What happened to my mother and father?

Mother, who'd mentioned a thousand times she hoped she'd never become helpless, became hopelessly senile.

Daddy, never known for nurturing, became her feeder, hair comber, bather, and launderer. He, who had rarely given, gave freely to his Lyda.

She who resisted taking entered a nursing home, regressed further until before her death she was frozen in a fetal position. Her death was a relief, for our bright Lyda had already been gone for ten years.

Lyda's Frank, my father, died of congestive heart failure when he was 98-1/2. Although Daddy's sight and hearing were aided mechanically at the last and his legs barely carried him to meals with the help of his walker, he was still strong willed, still the center of attention.

But after fifty years of Mother's adoration Daddy had reentry problems. His mind remained sharp, but his expectations became unrealistic, economic values – dated. And, most painfully, he distrusted views which differed from his own. He isolated himself from the shared truth which could have stabilized him, kept him centered.

We are much alike, my father and I, both fighters. But he clinched his fists at the path he was forced to walk until his last few years. I opened my clinched fists years ago and discovered another of God's truths. My hands could only be filled with His bounty when my fists opened to become supplicating bowls.

Yes, I felt his pain and isolation. Becoming old hurt him more than it has many others, for he lost his treasured 'ability to do' and his worth was built upon that. He, strangely, became my child, to sooth and help as often as possible. I spent several days with him each quarter although we lived a three-hour flight apart. But God checked me when I would consider him my responsibility.

As did I long ago, he longed for relief from his pain. He knew God held the key to his problem. He'd been flattened and lay before the Mousehole, the door to God's kingdom. How could I help him enter? What could I do?

"Love him," came a quiet answer. "Lift him to Me in your prayers. Be with him as much as you can, and always communicate Truth, for he needs to hear it. And, my child, you must guard against guilt for words or deeds done or undone. You have loved him well and wanted only his good. Your father's future has been shaped between him and Me. You bear no responsibility here. Trust me."

"Yes, Lord."

12

Pop-Pop, The Invisible

Pop-Pop, my husband's father, was actually tall and sandy-haired, but he was so low-profile he virtually disappeared. At times he'd be glimpsed moving silently through the house, turning burgers on the grill or repairing a lamp. The sounds of his sawing or hammering would occasionally drift in from his wood shop off the garage.

Dissimilar as unmatched bookends, Pop-Pop and Grammy – his tiny wife – were tall/short, quiet/noisy, loner/outgoer.

They had met in church in Los Angeles. Pop-Pop, the Swedish farm boy from Iowa, who had escorted his mother to California when she left his father – reasons unknown. Grammy, the Swedish orphan from Pennsylvania who was housed, clothed and brought to California by loving neighbors.

Pop-Pop apparently allowed Grammy to make all the decisions in their marriage. However that they would say grace, support the church and house his mother for life were given and his rare "No" was non-negotiable.

Retirement after forty years with the telephone company netted Pop-Pop time for golf, for cabinet building, and for neighborly assists such as retrieving a cat or repairing a roof. He loved to drive so they often took car trips, overnighting in moderately priced motels and enjoying eating out.

They often shared our home and we theirs, but this private man never spoke of his faith or his dreams and motivations...would be embarrassed should anyone ask him.

How did my new life make a difference in his? As far as I know, it didn't. Why have I included him in this narrative? Because his life and death became a visual sermon to me. I, so verbal, needed to see faith in action, faith without words.

Pop-Pop made his own sweet, black coffee several times a day, accompanying it with the Wall Street Journal, coffee cake or cookie. Most afternoons he shared his repast with an equally quiet neighbor who joined Pop-Pop for an hour of cribbage at the kitchen table. Pop-Pop always won. He also left the kitchen spotless.

Grammy became increasingly fragile, so Pop-Pop added cooking, housekeeping and nursing to his other skills. He was her "rock" through numerous surgeries.

He became our "rock", too, and lost his invisibility. The family considered him indestructible. Wasn't he in perfect health? our children's youngest grandparent?

And then the rock crumbled...

Surgeons spent fourteen hours repairing an aortic aneurysm. A lesser man wouldn't have lived, but Pop-Pop had to. Grammy needed him.

The next three years he strove to regain strength, speech and the use of his right hand. Perpetually tired, close to tears and embarrassed at his emotionalism, this silent man daily dressed, donned hat, coat and gloves, and walked his self-prescribed few blocks. He tried, unsuccessfully, to develop enthusiasm for once-loved food. Even his memory, finest in the family, was failing.

A fiftieth anniversary party honored two frail seniors. Vivid photographs of the event filled a white scrapbook which thereafter held honored place on the living room coffee table.

Pop-Pop's weight dropped from 180 to 115 pounds. His walks shortened to fifty yards a day. He never complained.

This man who had always been in the background became a giant in the family's eyes. We'd glimpsed the heart which motivated him, recognized his faith and uncomplaining *courage*.

A stroke came in the night and further damaged Pop-Pop's right side. Now he was hospitalized and unable to speak clearly or feed himself.

On taking leave of him on his last day, Grammy said, "Rest easy, Dear. You're in God's hands." Pop-Pop responded clearly for the first and last time since the stroke, "I know I am." Grammy was taken home, comforted.

That night Pop-Pop slipped away so gently his nurse believed him to be sleeping.

Gratitude for his release was the emotion which immediately swept our family. Escaping from his worn-out body was the only way Pop-Pop could be whole, well and free. We rejoiced for him.

Joy filled the house and was carried in our voices as we contacted distant family and friends. Those arriving for the funeral with, "We're so sorry," "You poor things," and "How sad it is", were clearly out of place.

Braced for grief at his father's death, Cliff was unprepared for lightness. Expecting to hate the open casket and social conventions of an earlier generation, he found they didn't matter – he had unrealized depth and strength within himself. Important and unimportant had become clearly identified.

Grammy became a new woman. Worry, which had drained her energies during Pop-Pop's illness, fled. Her step was lighter; she looked younger. Surrounded by family and friends who had known and loved her for years, tiny Grammy appeared queenly. Uplifted by their concern and prayers she wonderingly voiced, "I've never in my life felt so pampered and loved."

Although clothed in a new invisibility, Pop-Pop was still present, still loving us. It filled our conversation and warmed our hearts.

The night of the funeral our daughter slept in Pop-Pop's twin bed to be close to Grammy should she be needed. That night Carol felt Pop-Pop's presence in the room and his benediction upon her. Thanking God for this gift of His, she was forever changed.

Alone at home, filled to bursting with gratitude and praise, I whispered, "You did it, Pop-Pop! You managed to die as beautifully as you lived. I'm so grateful I could know you. Thank you." And, even more gently, "A special thanks to your Creator, too."

13

Grammy, The Kitchen Stove

Grammy, my husband's mother, was short and stocky with dark, tightly-curled hair. The first time I met her, she was welcoming, but her aproned figure returned quickly to the kitchen to finish preparing dinner. The delicious meal she brought to the lace-clothed table – meat, Irish and sweet potatoes, three vegetables, salad and relish plate, rolls and jam plus two kinds of dessert – was her idea of a company dinner. Everyone else labeled her dinners, "feasts."

Pop-Pop's mother, Grandma, helped in the kitchen, dined with us, and insisted upon doing the dishes alone. Her response to questions was usually a single syllable.

She dwelled in the privacy of her thoughts, the privacy of her room. It was easy to forget her presence in the modest, spotless house.

Whenever we visited, Cliff involved himself with his father. His mother involved herself with me.

Grammy was friendly and encouraging, interested in me, easy to love. I was drawn by her warmth as to an old-fashioned wood range in an otherwise cold kitchen. She radiated comfort, security, acceptance. That I should be subtly and repeatedly *burned* by this sweet woman was incomprehensible, but true.

Everything I did, and was, could be improved--my hair, wardrobe, activities. And I, believing authorities to be fair and logical – hadn't they always been – accepted her lovingly given suggestions as truth. It hurt to earn "D"s from her when I earned "A"s from others. Caring about her opinion, I tried even harder.

When Cliff and I announced our engagement, Grammy was plainly disappointed. I wasn't good enough for her only child. After our marriage I realized I had a *mother-in-law* problem. My role was to be a shield between Cliff and his mother. With me as the communicator, he didn't have to deal with her. I drew her artillery fire.

It's been said, "When a girl marries, she brings a son into the family; when a boy marries, he leaves his family." Not so with us. Following our marriage, ties to Cliff's family strengthened, ties to mine loosened.

His parents celebrated birthdays, anniversaries and holidays with us. Grammy bought us little presents, sent notes and cards and phoned often. I, not wanting them cut-off from their son, encouraged them.

Conversely, my parents rated presents, cards and holidays of little importance. They had too many projects on the fire to pay much attention to us. They didn't understand or exactly welcome Cliff into the family. We seemed to be interrupting when at their house. They seemed uncomfortable at ours. My ego was nose-diving without my noticing. Before, Mother and Daddy had been close and vocal in believing in me and my abilities. I believed in myself and it showed by the grades I earned. Now I was separated from my parents and from classes. My new schedule included unfamiliar tasks such as mopping, cooking and ironing men's shirts. Those who now graded me were a perfectionist husband and a manipulative mother-in-law. No "A"s from them.

Teaching at a local junior high buffered me for a year and a half, but pregnancy stopped my teaching.

Two small children, too little energy, too much to do, and too little emotional support forced me to yell, "Uncle."

I asked God for help, and the direction I was given was to phone Dr. Richard, our friend and psychiatrist, and book an appointment.

"What's the problem?", he asked.

"My mother-in-law," I answered. "I could keep my ship on course if it weren't for her. It takes me a week to recover from one phone call, but she calls me daily. We're together every two weeks. I'm 'sinking' with no time to recover between 'hits'."

"What does she do that bothers you so?"

"She sweetly tells me whatever I'm doing could be done a different way with more success.

If the children are outdoors, she asks if they have sweaters on. On hearing they don't, she suggests I take better care of them and see that they don them. If they're wearing sweaters, shouldn't I be concerned about their overheating? She lives forty-five miles from us against the hills; we live near the beach.

If I serve rice it could have been pilaf. If I wear pants it should be a dress. If I'd pay more attention to my windows and floors, the house would sparkle. You get the picture."

"Obviously she's a pro at manipulating you. She climbs on your ego in order to raise her own. You'll never be able to match her at this game, so don't try. But there are a couple of strategies you could adopt.

The more complete solution, but a time consuming one, is to go into therapy and learn how your psyche works. Alternately, you can use a simple tool to gain protection."

When I opted for the latter, he continued...

"You have reacted to this woman as though she were an adult authority. She isn't. She's a little child who's beating on your shins with a baseball bat. You wouldn't allow your children to do this to you, and you mustn't allow her to do it either.

Decide which area bothers you most and seal it off from conversation with her. If she hurts you most through the children, don't allow her to discuss the children with you. If you need more room, seal off the areas of food, or housekeeping, or your clothes. Seal off as much room as you need.

Whenever she turns to a sealed area, say, 'I don't wish to discuss this with you.' She will repeatedly attempt to open an area, and you must repeatedly refuse to let her. You are, thus, taking away her baseball bat. Try it. I think you'll find it to be all you need."

On the drive home I realized I'd been given much-needed protection. At last I could defend myself.

That evening I told Cliff of my session with Dr. Richard and of my hopefulness for the future. He shocked me with a quiet, "I won't let you treat my mother like that." Hurt, I lay awake. *Mother* had obviously been chosen over *wife*. What to do?

The next few days I was comforted by the new psychological shield in my arsenal. It was insurance which was never used, never needed.

Each time Grammy worked her wiles I saw her as a little girl trying to hit me, instead of as a rational authority. It made all the difference. That which had been unbearable was no longer of concern. Except...the few, short times business kept Cliff and me apart, she managed to make him see me through negative eyes, and then I threw dishes, beat my pillow and wept out my anger and frustration.

Years later this woman of average appearance told me her mother had once said, "You have such pretty hands it's too bad you can't hold them in front of your face all the time." She continued by holding out her arthritic hands for my inspection and saying, "It's too bad they're no longer pretty."

Grammy's mother and father had both died before she entered her teens. Her older brothers left, taking no responsibility for her. She was reared, but never adopted, by her across-the-street neighbors. No wonder she'd developed hurtful-to-others coping mechanisms.

Grammy was one of God's best learning tools. Had I not had her in my life I'd still be a crippled child. He used her to teach me to value myself, to evaluate criticism and to deeply love.

Most of the gifts Grammy hand-picked for Cliff and me were functional, but I remember the Christmas when my present was a pair of ornate figurines for our fireplace mantel.

Cliff and I preferred contemporary furnishings and had been slowly furnishing our living room, but the mantel was bare. We'd not yet found the right item or items to put upon it, nor did we yet have the funds to pursue the project.

Grammy was so proud of the dainty French court figures, frozen during a dance. She pointed out their painted fingernails, rouged cheeks, curled hair. I was aghast. How could we disappoint her by refusing this gift. We couldn't, obviously. I thanked her and set the figurines upon the narrow ledge.

After they'd gone, Cliff and I discussed the figurines. They appeared as impossible in our home to him as to me. They weren't even great porcelain, for which we might overlook divergent ambience, but inferior copies.

We apparently had three choices: to swallow our pride and let the figurines live permanently upon our mantel, to bring them out only when his parents visited, or to confront Grammy and Pop-Pop with the truth — we couldn't use them. The first choice we couldn't stand, the second was a lie, and the third would be very painful. We settled for the third.

I immediately shopped for something for the mantel which we both would enjoy, settling upon a pair of handsome brass Scandinavian candlesticks which we couldn't afford. They immediately took the figurines' place.

The subject of the missing figurines came up two weeks later. We brought them forth in their original wrappings and told Grammy and Pop-Pop how much we appreciated them. But, we continued, they'll look so much better in your home than in ours we're giving the figurines back to you. Was Grammy hurt? Yes. But she really loved those dainty people and kept them on her own mantel for years.

As she aged, Grammy mellowed; or did I?.

Shortly after Pop-Pop died, Grammy was diagnosed as having pancreatic cancer and needing nursing care. She obviously couldn't stay in California while we lived in Texas, so we brought her to the best local facility we could find. It was more than twenty miles from our home through the heart of Houston.

I was willing to give her time and attention because it was my duty, but God wouldn't have it. He dictated the terms whereby I could be with Grammy.

I could do nothing except for love – only what I wanted to do. And thus began the strangest year of my life.

During the year Grammy went from 110 to 70 pounds. The cancer couldn't be stopped, but her doctor rerouted her alimentary canal so she could continue to enjoy food. Later he radiated specific nerve endings so she could escape the pain which normally accompanies this killer.

Being in her room proved too hard on Cliff, so I went alone, making twice-weekly to daily trips to her bedside, fighting her battles and holding her hand. My writing time was lost to me, media appearances diminished, and homemaking efforts fell behind. When I mentioned needing at least cleaning help, Cliff volunteered his services. He said he could at least handle the housework while I was doing what he couldn't – helping his mother. Dear man. For a year I didn't touch a dust cloth, clean an oven or disinfect a toilet.

During that year Grammy and I grew together, enfolded by the most beautiful love imaginable. I became her "white knight," the one she depended upon and whom she loved without reservation. She became the only person I've ever found, besides God, who could accept all the love I had to offer. Parents, husband and children hadn't her capacity.

We hugged and giggled and shared. No longer daughter-in-law and mother-in-law, we became best friends. We talked often of her pending death, and joked about her going ahead to make sure heaven was clean enough for Cliff and me. She'd shape it up fast. She was comforted by the knowledge Pop-Pop awaited her.

I wept my tears as she was failing, but none at her death or Memorial Service Celebration amongst her dearest friends.

I miss this remarkable woman, think of her often, and still feel her warmth and love surrounding me.

14

⤼

Other "Mousehole"
Travelers

"The Drunkard"

Brian's escapades had enlivened bridge games and over-fence gossip for years. This occasional writer, nearly full-time tippler, was widely considered a ne'r-do-well. His wife, Edith, was considered a gracious, hard-working career woman, wife and mother. "What a pity," said the tongues, "She'd be so much better off without him, as would the girls."

Brian's drinking had been the catalyst which brought Edith to God's "Mousehole" eight years before. She gave away herself and her problem and gained the direction and strength to live fully – within the same circumstances which had previously proven unbearable.

Brian was only forty when his liver could no longer take the punishment. He was dying...without faith.

That Brian would accept God had been Edith's most fervent prayer, but the hoped-for had not happened. Time was running out. Praying yet again, Edith was directed to ask her town's three churches to join her in prayers for Brian's healing.

This was a small Ohio town with insular churches, each jealously guarding territory. They hadn't worked together on anything in her memory. Surely the two to which she didn't belong would refuse her request. But they didn't.

Brian was added to personal prayer lists all over town, and universal criticism was replaced by universal love.

When Brian crawled through the "Mousehole" and came forth a new man, the town rejoiced in his spiritual healing, and prayers of gratitude were raised.

No, he wasn't made physically strong. He died quietly, at peace with his Maker. But his death was victorious. It was used to heal pettiness, criticism and isolationism – to heal a town.

"The Priest"

Father Tom was a young Episcopal priest in an argumentative Colorado parish. He was blessed with sensitivity, brightness and a lovely wife and son. But the responsibilities of his office and the impossibility of pleasing parish officers so burdened him his smiles became few. As did Atlas, he carried the world on his back.

His wife, Ann, passed through the "Mousehole" when we lived across the street. She gave up the "dove" mask she'd donned for security and became the free, bouncy "fox terrier" she was meant to be.

But despite our prayers, Father Tom stayed unchanged. He was still bowed with his burden when they accepted a new parish in another state. Christmas notes became our only contact for years.

But then a convention in Minnesota made a personal visit possible. I'd known Ann was in poor health, but I didn't know until my visit she was dying from Lou Geirhig's Disease. Despite her wheelchair, crippled body and badly slurred speech, my "fox terrier" friend hadn't changed. Ann was still warm, witty and wonderful. We spent nearly two joyous hours laughingly bringing each other up-to-date.

Father Tom thought it a miracle I could understand Ann, as family had been translating her speech for the past six weeks. Understanding her words wasn't possible until I listened to her obliquely, as one sees pe-

ripherally. We thanked God for His gift of communication.

The change in Father Tom was the biggest miracle.
He had become mature, strong and free. His parish was
his joy; his congregation's love for him and Ann was
tangible everywhere. No long faces in this household;
all were victorious in Christ.

"The Cheerleader's Mother"

Marge was a generous friend, a fellow alto in the
church choir, and the busy mother of six.

Before the accident her oldest child, Debbie, had
been sixteen, blue-eyed, blond and bubbly – a pretty
high school cheerleader. After the drunk driver hit the
car in which she rode, Debbie was gone, her bruised
body a lifeless shell.

Debbie's memorial service was held at our church
on a weekday afternoon. The full choir had assembled
although tears muffled our voices. At the front was a
draped table upon which lay Debbie's Bible, her flute,
her cheerleader's hat and the collage she'd made in
Sunday School two days before – illustrating her hopes
and dreams.

On the front row sat her grieving family, heads
bowed, but not Marge's. Marge's head was up, her face
tear-stained but glowing, her bearing that of a soldier.

Behind her appeared to be the entire student body of the local high school – all truant.

Our young minister gave an inspired message of praise and thanksgiving. He spoke of Debbie's brief life and her glowing future. I saw the wonder in the faces of those fifteen through eighteen-year-olds – most unacquainted with church or faith.

God's music filled the sanctuary. Tears welled and overflowed.

Peace filled me and was immediately followed by the thought, had Debbie lived to be ninety she couldn't have been better used to reach the questing, the lonely, the lost. Was she not the lucky one – leaving so young to live with the Father? Think of the pain she'll miss!

As soon as I could see Marge in private, I asked about her regal bearing and strength at such a time.

She said she'd immediately hated and blamed the man who had killed her daughter. He had a long record of drunk driving arrests...should be locked-away for life. Her storming at this villain seemed to bring relief, but God wouldn't allow it. She was asked, "Will you forgive this child of mine and pray for him?"

"Please no, Lord, You've asked too much of me," she answered.

"And yet I ask it," He replied. "Will you forgive this child of mine and pray for him?"

"Yes, Lord, if you desire it," she responded in tears. "Give me the words and the strength." And He did. From that moment anger and hatred became peace.

Marge said she couldn't count the numbers of young people who came to talk of Debbie's death but stayed to ask the source of Marge's faith and amazing strength. She consoled those who came to console.

"The Agnostic"

My brother, Bill, left the church when he was thirteen. I can remember the exact moment. It was when our under-educated Sunday School teacher erroneously told the class, "You must choose between science and religion. They are mutually exclusive."

Bill chose science, shut off religious words thereafter, graduated from Cal Tech at twenty and died in his fifties a millionaire.

I, hearing the same message, procrastinated. I wasn't ready to make such a choice...was never again asked to.

Bill and I played and fought as children, double-dated in college, socialized as married couples, enjoyed arguing but remained friends. Anytime I spoke of spiritual matters he patted me, his little sister, on the head and dismissed my "fantasies."

Had he been happy, my prayers in his behalf would have been less frequent, but he wasn't. He gave everything to the job, little to his family, and too often looked to alcohol to solve his problems.

Where had I learned that when we pray for someone, we leave ourselves open to pain? In order for God to heal He must yank the rug of self-sufficiency from under the object of our prayer. Since caring places us on the same rug, we must willingly accept the pain of their fall.

But I also knew God chooses the least painful means each prayer can be answered, and God supports us with perspective and strength to stand firm – whatever happens.

Thus, when we heard Bill's surgeon had removed some cancerous tissue, it seemed apparent God was making His move. A second time, in another area of the body, unusual cells were excised. Bill called it minor; we accepted it so.

During a visit to California from Holland, where we lived for a time, I learned Bill was mid-way through a chemotherapy series. Lung cancer was the prognosis. Both he and his wife smoked.

I saw Bill briefly on the weekend when he was at home, but he forbad me to visit him in the hospital. His wife said he didn't allow anyone to visit him there. He looked exhausted and sick. When I checked with my Inner Guidance, I was told not to be concerned. Bill was on God's path to healing.

On my last night before returning to Europe John and I dined together then drove home past Uncle Bill's hospital. It felt right that we visit him. Without a word we simultaneously turned into the hospital chapel for prayer before ascending to his floor.

Bill's nurse said he needed visitors. Weak and teary, he was afraid of exposing his inability to cope. We went in. Our hour was spent in teasing Bill about his pajamas and the attractive nurses, in sharing with him our activities, in raising his spirits. Serious talk didn't belong. Because he said he'd welcome my return early the next day, before my flight, I left with hope.

The next morning Bill accepted my carefully selected spiritual books with no enthusiasm and said, "Jane, I'm not interested in your God. I've run my whole life without a God, thank you, and will continue to do so. I'm in a crazy race where chemotherapy and cancer are competing. I'm betting the chemotherapy will kill the cancer before I'm killed by either one of them...the odds aren't too bad." We embraced for the last time.

I left depressed until these words popped into my mind, "Do you think *you* are the only one who can speak for me? I have many messengers who are better equipped to speak to Bill than his sister. Trust me. He is in my care."

My prayers of thanks for God's care of Bill continued. He completed his medication series and went back to work part-time. We heard through others he seemed to be holding his own – was even getting tan – although he had limited lung capacity and tired easily.

At 3:00 am the phone jolted me from sleep and bed. John was calling Holland from California. A church friend of John's, a nurse who work-ed in Bill's cancer hospital's intensive care unit, reported Bill had just been admitted and attached to a lung machine. Prognosis? Bill's lung tissue had been destroyed by chemotherapy. He'd not leave there alive.

I wept and railed, angry at God for promising Bill's healing – spiritual if not physical – and not delivering on His word. I tried to pray, but words meant nothing. I asked for God's arms around me, but I felt nothing. Those became the most agonizing five minutes of my life.

My desperate prayers slowly turned into one amazing one. "It doesn't matter if I ever know of Bill's healing, Lord," I found myself praying. "Pride needed to know. I don't. As long as Bill is in Your arms, he's secure."

It was as though sunlight, warmth and comfort filled my dark room. I was back in God's pocket. My heart was full of rejoicing and thankfulness. "Bill is saved. Bill is saved. Bill is saved..."

I wrote the family the good news even though Bill still lived attached to machines, and could refute it. I received no external evidence to verify my inner knowledge, but I knew. Two weeks later he died, quietly.

Six months after his death we returned to the States. Then I learned the day before he died Bill had sent a company car so Daddy could visit him. Daddy and Bill had remained frustrated for a lifetime, each wanting to be told by the other he was okay. Their times together had rarely been enjoyable, but Bill spent their last hour lovingly telling Daddy all his pleasant memories of childhood and of the times they'd shared. He ended the visit with a smile and the words, "This isn't our last visit. I'll be seeing you."

Those aren't the words of an agnostic. They're the words of a believer. Hallelujah.

I feel closer to Bill than I did when he was alive and eagerly await our next time together. The impish little-sister in me longs to taunt, "I told you so!", but it's not necessary. He knows.

I would mourn the wasted years when he felt so poverty-stricken and I so blessed in God's kingdom, but they aren't important. We are together now, separated only by the thinnest veil. Thanks be to God.

Afterword

Picture a still pond deep in the forest. Decaying leaves partially float, whining insects strafe the surface, paw prints mark surrounding mud. A tiny spring of clear water feeds this pond, but sediment and debris have long since turned its water opaque and odorous.

My conscious mind mirrors this. Knowledge, emotion and habit muddy the Living Water, hiding eternal truth from me.

But God supplies the long straw through which I sip directly from the spring. The spring is truth, goodness and life. The straw is the gift of grace.

When I risk all on His direction, I may not reach the world's awards, but I never fail. When I choose the safe, logical position, I always stumble and fall.

After years of speaking rarely of the God which indwells and directs me, I was recently startled out of my silence. During a three-hour unscheduled visit with an almost stranger I found I'd lived through the solutions to one after another of her spiritual problems. That night I knew another book was required of me. This one.

"No, Lord. This doesn't make sense. I have other image areas lined up to research. Smart authors don't shift genre in mid-career. Now isn't the time for me to write this book. You know Cliff, our children, my father will be threatened if I'm honest. I know nothing but honesty is possible with you."

"Yes," came the gentle response, "I know all of the above. I'll handle them; trust me."

As I wrote these lines, *Through The Mousehole* seemed complete. Format, what to say where, how to say it has all been given. In less than five weeks this book sprang forth intact. It has rested in my files since 1988, awaiting the time for final edit and publishing.

A simple bout with breast cancer in 1990 left me asymmetrical but grateful for life, with no need to add to this story.

But, suddenly this fall, additional words are being called for.

Six months of undiagnosed intestinal malady has suddenly become terminal pancreatic cancer. With the verdict came two reactions. The first of profound relief since by this point my doctors were pretty much agreed that it was all in my head. It was nice to have my sanity verified.

My second response was to a beautiful image. A long line separated black on the bottom from glowing golden light on the top – the light representing God's gifts to me in this lifetime – people, projects, gifts of all manner and time. Not the least of which were my and Cliff's wonderful 45 year marriage. How could I who have been given so much whine about not receiving additional years of life? It would be like kicking God in the shins. Ingratitude and self-pity are clearly inappropriate both for me and for those who love me. If we keep the vision, the golden light of God's gifts will go on in others long after we are gone.

I don't know if there's an audience for my story of God's dealing, but it's unimportant. This slim volume will be published with my prayers that you who read it will find something of value here.

I've delighted in recording this journey, relearned vital lessons and experienced new perspectives – those beyond my grasp at the time they happened. I'm awed at His power to pour words through me, words which test true, and humbled I should be the one so chosen. An unexpected dividend is that the mention of this book's title opens fascinating conversations with unique people. It promotes deep sharing.

As you realize, this narrative isn't a treasure map you carefully follow – your prize *the kingdom of heaven*. There can be no map since each person's path is individually planned. *He who set the stars in the heavens* has a unique road for you to travel. If it should resemble my road, I'd be much surprised. Trust *your* road and Him.

If your terrain within The Kingdom is mountainous while mine is desert, your directions received from Scripture while mine come from Spirit, your rules the opposite of mine – no matter. The fruits of our lives verify us as His children and make us kin.

If you lie flat, glimpsing the Mousehole but afraid to enter, here's a welcoming hand. Come on in; the journey's exciting, and forgiveness and peace will accompany you.

If you stand erect and capable, not needy as I, congratulations. Thanks for your forbearance and for viewing my struggles with kindness.

None can see the road ahead – only the dust behind. I move one step at a time, stumbling often, trusting my Guide but needful of comradeship. If you're ahead of me on this mountain we scale, mark the pitfalls or throw me a rope. If you're behind, perhaps these words will bolster you for a few more steps.

Any truths you learn in your journey – share. New ways of seeing or saying or experiencing the nature of the One with whom we travel are invaluable to this alienated world. Make them known. We can never know enough about this beautiful, fascinating, upside-down, world we've reached **THROUGH THE MOUSEHOLE.**

To order additional copies of this or other books by Jane Segerstrom, please contact:

Triad Press
Post Office Box 42006
Houston, TX 77242, U.S.A.
713/978-7212 Phone
713/789-0424 FAX

Other titles include:

Look Like Yourself & Love It!, the 4-T Guide to Personal Style, Triad Press, 1980, ISBN 0-936740-06-X.

Style Strategy: Winning the Appearance Game, Triad Press, 1988, ISBN 0-936740-12-4.